LITTLE DARLING

Daryl Braithwaite and The Horses

Last Day of School

ISBN: 978-0-6489911-4-4
Little Darling: Daryl Braithwaite and The Horses is copyright Glen Humphries 2023

For more information (or to send oool memes email ghumphries26@gmail.com. If you loved this book so much that you want to buy some more copies then head over to my micropublishing site Last Day of School (find it at www.lastdayofschool.net). And maybe buy some copies of my other books. They're good, I promise you. And all so reasonably priced.

This book is copyright. All rights reserved. Except for private study, research, criticism or reviews, as permitted under the Copyright Act, no part of this book may be reproduced, stored in a retrieval system, or transmitted in any form or by any means without prior written permission. If you're thinking TL:DR, well just don't steal stuff from my book without giving me credit, okay? There's not much money in this book publishing caper to begin with, I don't need people to go stealing my stuff too. So be cool about it.

About the Author

Glen Humphries has been a journalist for a long, long time. Since 1994, in fact. He only stumbled into the trade, actually. He wanted to be a dentist or a doctor because he figured they made heaps of cash, but his life course was changed when he did a week's work experience at a local newspaper in Year 11. After that he went to uni in Wollongong and then pestered the *Illawarra Mercury* until they relented and gave him a job. Because this is the place where you're supposed to say things like this, he has won several awards for writing. One of his books, *The Slab*, was the national winner in the Gourmand World Cookbook Awards. This was despite the fact that it's not actually a cookbook at all. He's been writing and self-publishing books since 2017. You can find them all at his site Last Day of School (lastdayofschool.net). Why does he do it? Well, he's quite a book geek for starters. Also, he got sick of wishing someone would write a book on topic X so he decided he'd do it himself. Since then, he looks at his sales numbers and has realised that, in some cases, there's a very good reason why no-one had written a book on topic X. No worries, he still likes looking at all the books he's written lined up on the downstairs shelves. He once interviewed Daryl Braithwaite over the phone and, after it was finished, they had a long chat. Most musicians *never* do that. He's old enough to have bought *Edge* when it first came out – on vinyl. He tried to learn guitar several times but lacks the patience. And once his teacher showed him power chords, he had all he needed to know. His CD shelves are in alphabetical order but his vinyl is organised by artist. He can't explain why. He has never sung along to *The Horses* in public.

Also by Glen Humphries and published by Last Day of School (www.lastdayofschool.net) unless otherwise noted

Friday Night at the Oxford
Sounds Like an Ending: Midnight Oil, 10-1 and Red Sails in the Sunset
Healer: The Rise, Fall and Return of Tumbleweed
Alright!: Queen at Live Aid
Lull City: The Wollongong Music Scene 1955-2020
Biff: Rugby League's Infamous Fights (published by Gelding Street Press)
The Slab: 24 Stories of Beer in Australia
James Squire: The Biography
The Six-Pack: Stories from the World of Beer
Beer is Fun
Night Terrors: The True Story of the Kingsgrove Slasher

For Josie, who knows about The Horses, even though she was born more than two decades after it was released.

Little Darling

Introduction

Normally, when people drive by a council gang doing maintenance on the side of the road, they don't give them a second glance. All they see is the hi-vis clothing and whether the sign says "stop" or "go".

But just maybe for a short period in the now defunct northwest Melbourne shire council of Bulla, things were a little different. Maybe, when drivers – usually female – went past a certain road gang, they did a double take at one particular worker. "No," they said to themselves, "that can't be him. Why would he be out here on a shovel?".

They might have remembered the face from watching *Countdown* every Sunday night. Or maybe it was the album covers they remembered. Perhaps their younger self had a poster of him on their bedroom wall.

They drove by sure their eyes were playing tricks on them. Sure that the man in the poster on their teenage wall they stared at while laying on their bed wasn't the same man they just saw. "It sure was an uncanny likeness though," they thought to themselves. "He must get told all the time he looks like that singer."

It wasn't a lookalike. It was him. And his co-workers on the road gang were just as surprised to see him turn up for work one day, saying the dole office sent him here. Well, the older guys were surprised; the ones who remembered his bare-chested, satin baseball jacket years in the 1970s. The younger ones, well, he had been a bit before their time. And the man himself wasn't likely to brag about his glory days, trying to big-note himself. For a guy who had spent almost a decade being pursued by hordes of screaming teenage girls he was remarkably grounded.

Those older guys, they ended up helping the guy out. They didn't have many options other than being out there in all kinds of weather digging holes and laying bitumen. But him, well, he had a talent. The last decade proved that. So they asked him one question – "what the hell was he doing here?".

1

Born on January 11, 1949, that makes Daryl Braithwaite a Capricorn – just like Jesus and Elvis. Not that he necessarily has anything else in common with either of those two people – except maybe a period in 1970s Australia when people would refer to him by his first name alone and others knew who you were talking about.

Daryl and his twin brother Glenn (who must surely be sick of being asked "hey, are you related to that guy who sings *The*

Horses?") grew up in South Yarra, in their grandmother's house. They played cowboys and Indians in a nearby park for hours before graduating to war games as soldiers down near the train line. They took it all very seriously indeed – their aunt bought them camouflage gear, helmets and walkie-talkies.

When he went to high school, he found himself in the same class as a girl named Olivia Newton-John (yes, that one). They were soon holding hands. "She was one of the prettiest girls in the class – we were 11 or 12 I think," he said. "I don't know how, we must have sat next to each other and thought 'oh yeah, that's good' and we were talking and then we held hands and then it was all over."

In the years since, he's been asked about her a lot more than her about him. He even wrote her entry in *Rolling Stone*'s 50 Greatest Artists of All Time. (she came in at No20. Outrageously Daryl couldn't crack the top 50). He included a class photo with the piece that shows them in the same row; Daryl shorter than everyone in the row, Olivia standing out just off-centre of the frame showing his assessment of her being "the prettiest in the class" was quite accurate.

Olivia remembered dating the guy who went on to adorn the bedroom walls of many a teenage girl. "He was so cute," Newton-John remembered. "He's still cute, but he was a very cute little boy."

And the rest of the kids in that photo probably grew up to bore people by telling them how they were in the same class as Olivia Newton-John *and* Daryl Braithwaite.

In 1963, the family packed up and moved to the beachside Sydney suburb of Coogee. Braithwaite and his brother had already been singing in the school choir before the move. "I think both Glenn and I got singing from our dad," Braithwaite said. "Mum used to say he would sing at the drop of a hat. He was a great singer."

It wasn't until the move to Sydney that music became a key focus in his life. That along with a love of surfing led to a less than stellar high school career, with his attention very much elsewhere.

So he left at Year 10 and was pushed into a fitting and turning apprenticeship at Cockatoo Island at the end of Parramatta River. "I went to it because mum and dad – especially dad – was frustrated because I wasn't doing well at school because I had no interest. So I accepted the trade and went along with it."

Though he didn't seem to take the apprenticeship any more seriously than he had school work. If he looked out at the beach on the way to work and the waves were pumping, well, he just wouldn't turn up for work that day. By his own estimate, he probably took a 'surf day' once a fortnight.

So it was no surprise that one day he was called in to see the boss. At the end of the day, they reached a compromise – he got the papers that said he'd completed his apprenticeship and they got to replace him with someone who turned up for work every day.

"I wasn't overly impressed with fitting and turning," Braithwaite said. "I did it as a trade but I was very happy to leave and go off and do this thing called music."

2

And Daryl soon got the chance to do "this thing called music" in a big way. While he had been singing in bands while working at Cockatoo Island, they weren't anything serious – he later described them as "hobby bands".

But then a guitarist named Clive Shakespeare approached Braithwaite and asked if he'd join his band, Sherbet. The band had started in 1969 – though by the time they became a success a few years later,

Shakespeare would be the only original member.

When Braithwaite joined in March 1970, the band had already released the single *Crimson Ships*, with original vocalist Dennis Laughlin. Establishing a trend the band would follow for the first two years of their career – it was a cover. The song appeared on an album released by Badfinger in 1970, meaning the original was still available when Sherbet chose to release their cover.

It wasn't a great debut and didn't set the charts on fire, which was handy. Releasing a debut single and then changing your singer would have been confusing for those who did buy the record.

The first two singles released with Braithwaite's vocals were also covers. The first, *Can You Feel It Baby*, was meant as a duet for a male and female vocalist, Braithwaite using his impressive falsetto to sing the girl parts while new keyboard player Garth Porter took the male parts.

The second single was *Free The People*,

chosen because it had a tuba part – an instrument played by bassist Bruce Worrall. That could well have been the first time a pop band chose a song because it had tuba in it. The tunes impressed the public enough to reach the top 20 in the charts (at No16 and No18 respectively).

The third Braithwaite single, released in April 1972, was also written by someone outside the band. *You're All Woman* was penned by Ted Mulry, who gave the song to the band after a "drunken evening", according to the band's 1975 greatest hits collection.

By this time, the Sherbet line-up had stabilised with the addition of drummer Alan Sandow and bassist Tony Mitchell. They also discovered they could write their own songs, evidenced by the next single *You've Got The Gun*, written by the pair of Porter and Shakespeare with the help of Braithwaite. Despite it being better than the first four singles, it didn't make the top 20.

These three singles appeared on the

band's 1972 debut album, somewhat pretentiously called *Time Change … A Natural Progression*. Of the 10 songs on the album, six were written by the band.

In the late 1960s and early 1970s, there was a national band competition sponsored by confectionary maker Hoadley's. In what is a clearly unfair decision, bands who already had a record contract were allowed to enter the Hoadley's Battle of the Sounds.

Sherbet came second in 1971, losing out to Adelaide outfit Fraternity (featuring a pre-AC/DC Bon Scott). Figuring they could go one better, Sherbet entered again in 1972 – which turned out to be the last year of the competition.

They took out first prize, which was a trip to LA, along with $1000. The band was more interested in the cash than the trip, because they were keen to buy a better van so they could tour around Australia.

At the time they entered, Sherbet was not the band we know of now; the act trailed by screaming girls wherever they went. That debut album wouldn't climb higher than No66 on the charts. But things changed in 1973, possibly sparked by the Battle of the Sounds win. Though the band had one more cover to release, the quite unnecessary *Hound Dog* "especially for our Melbourne audience". If that was the case, it suggests Melbourne music fans were not always ahead of the game.

3

By the time the second album, *On With The Show*, was released in November 1973 (just in time for Christmas!), the heavy reliance on cover versions was a thing of the past. While there was only nine tracks on the album – guys, double figures really is the minimum number of songs for a long player – they were all originals. Well, except for a nine-and-a-half minute cover of Graham Nash's *Chicago*. That's nearly seven minutes longer than Nash's version, and you can hear the padding.

Shakespeare and Porter were still developing as songwriters, as shown by the album opener *We Can Make It Right*, which takes the cheesy option of mentioning each band member in the lyrics. For example, "Here's our potion if you've got the blues/Alan's got a beat we're gonna use" followed by an obvious drum break.

But among stuff like that was the pair's sultry *Jubilee Morning* and their first bona fide hit *Cassandra*, written mostly by Porter. Not that he knew a Cassandra; he'd read something about the Greek goddess and the name appealed to him.

The charts rewarded Porter's love song to a goddess, making it the band's first top 10 single, landing at No5. But there was much more impressive stuff to come for Sherbet.

A year later they released *Slipstream*, an album the band has Sister Janet Mead to thank for its quality. In 1974, the good Sister released a weird prog-rock/pop cover of *The*

Lord's Prayer. God was obviously on her side because it was a hit and made enough money for her record company Festival to upgrade its studio facilities to a 24-track recorder. So that's where Sherbet went to record *Slipstream*, which showed an uptick in sound quality compared to their earlier stuff.

There was also the fact the band had a bit of time to work on the album. Before this, Porter said the band was always in a rush because there was always one tour or another to do so the game plan was to get in and out of the studio as quickly as possible. But on *Slipstream* they were able to take their time.

The change of studio and the extra time paid dividends. The album – made up of nothing but original compositions – went to No3 and spawned two top five singles *Slipstream* and *Silvery Moon*. The former featured an ear-catching theremin-like keyboard line while the latter is unapologetically schmaltzy but still surprisingly endearing.

Little Darling

There was also a song that, given Sherbet's cleanskin image, seemed to slip in under the radar. *Handy Mandy* is clearly an ode to Mandrax – a well-known drug of the 1970s known by the slang name 'mandies' (and also quaaludes). They were initially used as a sleep aid until hipsters in the 1960s and '70s found they were fun to take.

If there were any doubts about the subject matter of the song, lyrics like "I love the way you take me down" and "turning hours of sadness into joy" are pretty strong indicators. Yet despite this – and the drug bust of Mitchell along with an incident where the punch at a Sherbet promo function was spiked with LSD – somehow the band managed to retain a squeaky clean image. Oh, and with all those screaming females following them everywhere, you can't expect me to believe the band didn't choose to get exceptionally friendly with some of them.

In the early days, Sherbet's career got a boost from their appearance in a TV ad for cologne. In fact some naysayers at the time felt their early fame was more a result of the ad rather than their music. It was a black and white ad for 4711 Ice Cologne, where a sweaty Braithwaite sings the jingle ("4-7-11, Ice down" are the only words I can make out), while a woman keeps getting ice cubes thrown onto her bare back. Porter is the only other band member who makes an appearance splashing some of the product on his face.

The band also appeared in a more risqué ad for the original 4711 cologne, which featured a naked woman getting a curious amount of pleasure from pouring the stuff all over herself. A drop trickles down between her breasts as Braithwaite sings "Splash it on, little girl, and everywhere it touches is refreshed". Though, to be fair, it's doubtful anyone watching the ad was paying attention to the guy doing the singing.

4

Everyone has a photo of embarrassing fashions or haircuts hidden away in a photo album or a shoe box jammed up the back of the closet. If we choose, we can keep it tucked away from the world, or maybe only show it to a few trusted friends. But we can at least ensure it doesn't end up in the public domain where everyone can see it, forever.

Braithwaite and the rest of Sherbet never had that luxury. Each fashion faux pas is out there in public for all to see. And the band was big in the 1970s, so there are a lot of cringeworthy fashions hanging around. Case in point is the cover of that *Slipstream* album, where the band is wearing make-up that looks as though it were applied by someone in an amateur theatre company. With their eyes closed. Why a band with several handsome faces in it saw the need to ruin the look by slapping on some make-up is odd. Maybe they figured they were going to be a glam band. Fortunately, they'd ditched the make-up by the time they had to take photos for the next album.

It's even scarier when you open up the *Slipstream* gatefold sleeve (surprisingly, almost all of Sherbet's releases were graced with a gatefold sleeve). There's the band with their make-up again, only this time the photo is much larger, so you can really see how bad the make-up truly looks. It's Sandow – dead centre of the photo – who comes out the worst. With eye shadow and black lipstick along with eyes seemingly caught mid-blink, he appears wasted. Which maybe was the only way he'd let the band make him look so foolish.

And we haven't even touched on the '70s fashion yet. Shakespeare has white flares and a blue satin kimono thing, while Mitchell is sporting white pants, knee-high black boots, a green satin jacket and white vest knotted at the front with the ties hanging down. There's also a jumpsuit or two in there as well. In the gatefold, some are looking more sedate in 1970s-era jackets and suits, while Porter has a low-cut, ball-hugging aqua leotard topped with a white jacket. Mitchell has kept that weird vest thing he had on the cover, but paired it with a green satin jacket and red satin pants. He looks like an upside-down traffic light.

Of course there are shockers on the other album covers. Testicle-separating jeans, bare hairy chests, a drummer inexplicably wearing nothing but a pair of brown underpants, more kimonos and those ubiquitous satin baseball jackets that Porter brought to the band. He'd found one at an op shop and told Richard Tyler, who was making clothes for the band, to knock up a few more for him. "It really took hold," he said. "Everybody in the band was having them made up to their own requirements."

Then there are the clips from *Countdown*. There are too many to mention so let's limit ourselves to their debut with *Silvery Moon*. Shakespeare has gone for blue pants and a red shirt with a black and yellow striped scarf – nothing matches anything else he is wearing. In his red-and-white striped jacket and pants, Braithwaite looks like a candy cane. Porter appears to be wearing women's blue satin sleepwear. As for Mitchell, his outfit is just eye-scarring. It's a leopard-print jacket with knee-length pants. The jacket comes with a stand-up collar that goes halfway up his skull. From the knees down he wears green socks that match his green shirt. One can only assume he didn't look in a mirror before he walked out onstage.

But the image that will dog the band forever is the nude photo shoot mistakenly credited to *Cleo* magazine. It wasn't one of that magazine's popular male centrefolds, rather it was taken by Lewis Morley for *POL* magazine, which was running nude blokes in their centrefold before *Cleo* cottoned onto the idea.

Morley – who also took that iconic nude shot of Christine Keeler sitting on a chair – got the band to strip off their duds in 1972 and cuddle up. Members' arms are around others' shoulders, legs are draped over each other, with Mitchell lying on his stomach having slid between some of those legs. All the sensitive bits are covered up, though Braithwaite's rather hirsute groin area is clearly visible.

There is a more embarrassing variation of this image, which features the addition of soap suds. Several members have taken to manspreading, with some of those soap suds covering up dicks. The most overt is Sandow whose legs are spread wide with just a handful of suds to avoid any blushes.

The band has little hope of seeing these

images quietly fade away. The former image has now been made into a jigsaw puzzle, while Morley has donated other images to both the National Portrait Gallery (which includes a photo of the band with stockings pulled over their heads like 1970s bank robbers) and the Art Gallery of NSW. So those images are likely to be around forever.

5

The TV series *Countdown* came along at exactly the right time for Sherbet. In fact it was like they were made for each other.

The legendary pop music show, which was must-see TV every Sunday night for more than a decade, started out in November 1974 as a batch of six half-hour shows. None of which were hosted by Molly Meldrum, by the way. Radio DJs did the job back then. Molly wouldn't turn up until the following year when the show moved to the hour-long colour format everyone remembers. At a time when each state had its own radio stations and there was no such thing as syndication, *Countdown* had a national reach. Get the chance to play on the show and kids from Sydney to Perth would see you. It's little wonder the show quickly developed the power to push songs onto the charts.

At the time *Countdown* debuted, Sherbet was on the rise and popular with teenage girls – who were a huge chunk of the TV show's viewership. So it made sense to have them appear on the show, which of course then helped raise Sherbet's profile.

It's surely no coincidence that the first song the band released after *Countdown*'s debut – the single-only *Summer Love* – was Sherbet's first No1 single. Not even the fact the was released in March 1975, when summer was over, got in the way of the tune's success. Nor did it hurt that Braithwaite's nan lived around the corner from Meldrum and would pop round and demand he play more of her grandson's band.

Sherbet was there in *Countdown*'s first colour episode and would become regular guests in both that incarnation and when they turned into The Sherbs. If that wasn't enough exposure, Braithwaite often got tapped on the shoulder to fill in a guest host role.

Once he was tapped on the shoulder midway through the 100th show in 1977, because Molly was wasted. Molly himself didn't deny the fact but claimed it was a result of combining Valium – given to him backstage to calm his nerves after a hectic week – and a vodka and orange from Renee Geyer.

He was soon out of it, mumbling even more than usual, almost falling asleep on camera and needing the help of performer John Paul Young to introduce the next segment. While that segment – a pre-recorded interview with Elton John – went to air, Meldrum was yanked offstage and

Braithwaite and JPY were told they had to host the remainder of the show.

"John and I were both mates of Ian's, so we thought we could go and have a chat to him and sort things out," Braithwaite remembered. "But we went in there and he was just so angry. He swore and swung a punch at me and I remember thinking 'Fuck this'. We ended up doing the last 10 minutes of the show on our own."

For many viewers too young to understand the effects of drugs and alcohol, Meldrum's behaviour might have gone unnoticed. But those older teens knew he'd taken something – either accidentally or intentionally.

"What a night it's been," Braithwaite told the teenaged crowd. "Listen, Ian Meldrum has been exhausted. Completely out of his … He's had enough and he's gone, but he said to say thanks for everyone coming in tonight."

Despite what happened backstage between Braithwaite and Meldrum it didn't harm the band's relationship with *Countdown*, appearing on the show a number of times after that.

As an aside, *Countdown*'s reputation for breaking acts isn't ironclad. While bands like Sherbet were pushed up the ladder of fame, for others an appearance on *Countdown* didn't result in much of anything happening. Looking through the schedule of episodes, there are bands names popping up that make you think "who the hell was that?".

One such act was White Xmas, the poor man's Pseudo Echo, who appeared 'live' on the show in 1987 performing the tune *Pearl Necklace*. While some brave souls volunteered to dance on the checkerboard dance floor in front of the band – though probably not aware of the sexual innuendo of the song – most of the audience stood around the edges, arms folded waiting for the band to get off the stage. Accordingly, White Xmas never set the world on fire.

Anyone remember Talk That Walk? They too appeared on *Countdown*, playing their song *Surface Tension*. They were a band who obviously had a few Boom Crash Opera records in their collection – because they totally swiped that band's drum sound, as well as a few other things.

A year earlier Billy Miller from one-hit wonders The Ferrets, turned up with his new band The Spaniards. Judging by Miller's performance on *Countdown* he had been studying the book *101 Rock Guitarist Moves*.

While their tune *What Can I Do* was catchy it still didn't propel them to success. Though the song was briefly propelled to No55 on the charts.

In '86 the terribly-named John Justin and Thunderwings appeared twice on *Countdown*, performing *Flash King Cadillac* and *Justice*. Listening to the first song, it's hard to understand why they asked him back a second time. If you've never heard this band before, I recommend you keep it that way.

Through the mid-80s Melbourne act Geisha kept on appearing on *Countdown*, but it never translated to national success. While singles climbed high in their hometown charts, nationally they didn't do a whole lot. And they had their chances – their record label released eight singles in two years.

As these examples show, a spot on the country's premier music show wasn't a guarantee of success on its own – you had to have something else going for you.

6

Most people think Braithwaite's solo career started in 1988 with the release of the *Edge* album. But that was actually the third time his solo career started. The first time was, oddly enough, in the mid-1970s when he was still member of Sherbet.

It wasn't Braithwaite thinking the Australian music scene needed more of him than it was getting with Sherbet; the whole thing was Shakespeare's idea.

"I think it might have been along the lines

of 'I've come up with this idea, Daryl. You don't have to go with it but maybe if you record solo just to see how it would work'," Braithwaite told podcaster Sean Sennett. "We never ever talked about whether it would jeopardise the band – that didn't come into it. It was just an adjunct to what Sherbet was doing."

Though in time, his solo success would spark unfounded rumours he was considering ditching Sherbet.

Braithwaite had dabbled outside the band before this – in 1973 he took a role in a short-lived production of The Who's *Tommy*, alongside Coleen Hewitt, Billy Thorpe and Doug Parkinson.

In 1974, he released his first solo single – a cover of *You're My World*. It went to No1 for three weeks. This was when Sherbet had yet to reach that illustrious chart position themselves.

Over the next four years Braithwaite released a handful of solo singles – the first four of which landed in the top 10. They were ultimately collected (along with all the B-sides) on a 'best-of' album in 1978 – right around the time Sherbet was drawing its last breaths.

There didn't seem to be any concern from the band that having his solo stuff and Sherbet stuff out there at the same time might be saturating the market and risking people getting sick of them.

In fact it seemed quite the opposite. Some of his singles were written by members of the band, who would also play on them (song credits also show a guitarist named Ian Moss, which could well be the same one from Cold Chisel). Several times *Countdown* features both a solo performance from Braithwaite and one from Sherbet.

The 1970s were also a time when compilation albums were gaining in popularity, and it wasn't unusual to find Sherbet and Braithwaite songs on the same disc. Including the now-infamous *Ripper* compilation, where their names – along with those of 14 other acts – were painted on a woman's bare butt cheek.

At the time, the market saturation didn't actually seem like a bad idea at all. It came right at the beginning of Sherbet's peak in popularity – who knows, it may have even caused it. For three years in a row from 1977, Braithwaite was named King of Pop in the *TV Week* awards (this was back when a TV guide was something people would actually buy). The band actually did much better – winning Best Pop Group an impressive seven years running from 1973.

But it was really from the mid-1970s that things reached a peak for Braithwaite and the band. It was a time when the band had to leave big gigs in armoured cars after getting sick of waiting fans wrecking their cars by jumping on them.

To see evidence of this crazy rush of fame you only need to watch Braithwaite's *Countdown* appearance where he sings *You're My World*. He walks down the stage wearing a lavender satin suit coupled with a very wide-collared purple shirt (unbuttoned almost to the waist, naturally). He heads down a small set of stairs to a catwalk that takes him out into the crowd, whose heads are waist height to him.

Once he stops at the end, the hands of any teenage girls in proximity start reaching out for him, wanting to hold his hand or caress that lovely satin suit. Sometimes he politely has to pull his hand out of their grip. On one occasion he reaches down to his right to touch someone's hand, only to find himself almost yanked into the crowd. It's such a strong tug that he actually disappears out of the camera shot. When he frees himself, he gives the girl a brief look as if to say "hey, not cool" before remembering he's on TV and cracking a smile.

He learned his lesson; after that moment he stopped reaching out for anyone's hand. The rest of the appearance is made up of Braithwaite at a marina – for some odd reason – wearing a facial expression that *Countdown* biographer Peter Wilmoth said made him look "very much not in love with the person whose world he wanted to be part of". Then he takes off his shirt and goes sailing, perhaps to escape the screaming girls for a bit.

You know you've made it as a pop star when girls want to touch you and pull you into the crowd. It was a similar story for the rest of Sherbet too. Sandow had compared their peak to The Beatles, where the girls were screaming so loudly the band couldn't hear themselves play. "For a long time it just went too far," he said. "We could have played anything and it wouldn't have mattered."

Mitchell remembered the obsessed girls got so bad that they had to bring in that armoured van to get them in and out of gigs.

Porter once found himself at the bottom of a football-style scrum of girls – and not in a good way. "It was at one of our gigs when we ran out to leave, but I forgot something and had to run back to the dressing room, only to emerge later and find all the security gone," he said. "I was immediately swamped and had all these girls on top of me."

7

With pop bands, you never really know how long they will last. So record companies look to wring as much money out of them as they can. In most cases, that means releasing a greatest hits collection, getting another hit of revenue from songs that had already been released.

So in mid-1975, with Braithwaite's solo career flying and the band's next album a few months away, their label looked to milk the cash cow that was Sherbet, releasing a greatest hits album.

This was despite the fact the band had really only had three hits at the time – if you define "hit" as a song that reached the top 10. Those hits that appeared on the album were *Cassandra*, *Slipstream* and *Silvery Moon*. If there were ever any doubts Sherbet didn't have enough hits for a greatest hits release, they had to bulk out the album with a handful of B-sides among the 14 tracks. And there's no way you can consider a B-side a "hit". Ironically, some of the band's biggest hits would come after the release of this greatest hits package.

The plan paid good dividends – the collection of songs (which most fans already had) went to No1 and paved the way for the band's new album.

And, for an act most people saw as a straightforward pop band, that new album was a surprisingly ambitious release. Who expects a pop act at the height of their fame to release a concept album?

Yet that's what *Life … Is For Living* was.

It even opened with a two-minute sound collage called *Arrival*, which tracked the history of Earth – including digeridoos and birds tweeting before giving way to axes and chainsaws cutting down trees, phones ringing and missiles launching. "Nobody went that far," Porter told Debbie Kruger. "Nobody [made] a sound effect montage of the evolution of man on Earth. Never in the history of recorded music has a popular band put such an incredibly left-field concept as the first track!"

The band had toyed with a concept album before – the first three tracks of *Slipstream* are interconnected. But they stretched things a bit further with *Life … Is For Living*.

Still, they managed to carry it off on what is a somewhat under-rated album. And the weird sound effects and addition of brass, flute and vibes didn't alienate the fans; the album went to No3 and the singles *Life* and *Only One You*, went to No4 and No5 respectively.

It truly seemed that Sherbet could do no wrong.

Around this time the band was painted as being in a fierce rivalry with Skyhooks, the other big band on the scene at the time. "In Australia over the past three months," Molly Meldrum wrote in a magazine column in 1975, "two amazing armies have been building up for a confrontation which could make the American Civil War look like kindergarten playtime. It was only recently that among thousands of pop fans in this country, especially on the female side, an incredible split has developed – you were either a hardcore Sherbet fan or a fanatical Skyhooks follower, and never the twain shall meet!"

It was all rubbish – Skyhooks' manager Michael Gudinski and Sherbet's Roger Davies were friends and the pop band often helped Skyhooks land gigs. But both bands loved it because it kept their names in print.

A rumoured tussle of a different sort

happened between Braithwaite and AC/DC's Bon Scott. The story goes that both bands were at the *TV Week* King of Pop awards show and Scott got rather drunk backstage. According to Mick Wall's AC/DC bio happy drunk Bon turned into angry drunk Bon, and he inexplicably grabbed a cooked turkey, poured champagne into its backside and then used it as a drinking vessel.

When it was empty, he pissed into the bird and then handed it to Braithwaite, who happened to be walking past. He took a swig and then spat it out in disgust.

It's a story that doesn't ring true, given that Scott was usually the victim of his drunk shenanigans. Also, when asked about the story, Braithwaite said it never happened and that Scott didn't have the kind of cruel streak the joke required.

Braithwaite has known Scott since the early days of the band, when they were honing their act at a Sydney club called Jonathan's. "We had a residency with

Fraternity and Bon was the singer in Fraternity we had some great times," Braithwaite said. "Bon was very quiet as I remember. Not shy – I just remember he kept to himself – but we were friends."

So there was no turkey drinking – and no Beatles vs Stones like battle with Skyhooks either.

8

Not long after the release of *Life … Is For Living* something happened that seemed to be the death knell for the band. Shakespeare – who had been co-writing the band's songs with Porter – had enough and quit. The reasons for the walk-out vary. It has been suggested there were issues within the band, with Shakespeare telling *RAM* at the time that he was "sacked". Though in later years Shakespeare said the pressures of Sherbet's fame just got too much to handle.

"I couldn't even go out the front of my house because there were all these girls just hanging on the fence," Shakespeare said. "There was always a deadline for Garth and me – another album, another tour. When it did finally end, I was relieved more than anything because I had had enough.

"I left the band early in 1976 for reasons I don't want to discuss fully … but let's just say I wasn't happy about where all the money went."

He'd try to start up a solo career, releasing the rocky single *I Realise* but things stalled after that, most likely because of feared confusion with singer William Shakespeare (real name: John Cave), who had a few hits around the same time. Instead, Shakespeare moved into record production, going on to co-produce Paul Kelly's debut solo album *Post*.

The last Sherbet song Shakespeare played on was the non-album single *Child's Play*, written as the theme for a kids TV show that was never made. It came with perhaps the oddest video the band ever shot. With the band set up in some sandhills, it has a Monkees vibe as the five guys get dressed up in 1800s military garb and muck about – sometimes chasing a girl in a bikini. It's probably the only time in the 1970s the band had to chase a woman, usually it was the other way around.

Normally, when a band loses one of its songwriters it results in a reduction in quality. But for Sherbet, the opposite happened. They brought in a new guitarist in Harvey James, and bassist Mitchell stepped into the breach to help Porter. And one of their first efforts came about while they were sitting in the music room of Porter's house in Rose Bay.

Mitchell came up with a slinky bassline (that surprisingly still hasn't been used as a sample by any Australian hip-hop or dance acts) and they built a song around it. A song inspired by manager Davies telling them they should write a song about cricket – after all this was a band that reportedly carried a cricket kit with them on tour.

That song was of course, *Howzat*, and it still causes Porter to cringe. "The lyrics are appalling," he said. "And that was all me. I'm the guilty party. I suppose they're part of the package of the song now, but when I read them in black and white, I think, 'Oh my God, a six-year-old could have written that'."

Porter may have hated it but Australia loved it – Howzat became the band's second No1 single. It hit that same spot in New Zealand, went top 10 in the UK and South Africa and was the only Sherbet single to chart in the US, where it reached No61.

The accompanying album – also called *Howzat* – showed no signs of missing Shakespeare either. Sherbet never made a uniformly strong album; each release had some dud tracks on it (one of the reasons such a popular band never features in any of those Top 100 Australian albums polls). And *Howzat* was no different, though at least they generally stuck the duds – the weird country/yodel-inspired *Can't Find True Love* and the tacky vaudeville of *I'll Be Coming Home* – at the end. In terms of changing songwriters, it was a pretty seamless transition – and *Howzat* ended up being the band's only No1 Australian album. The back cover and gatefold featured the band in an animated hot air balloon. The satin baseball jackets were still there and new boy Harvey decided it would be cool to wear a pith helmet. God only knows why.

The song and album created enough buzz that the band made the cover of the most definitely not music-orientated magazine *The Bulletin*. The news magazine suggested Sherbet were at the vanguard of Australian bands set to make waves overseas – especially in the UK.

"In recent months Australasian rock has begun to surface as a major force with the emergence of bands like AC/DC, Little River Band and Split Enz," wrote *The Bulletin*'s Camilla Beach. "And spearheading this invasion is Sherbet, the first new

Australian band to break into the British charts since the Bee Gees turned disaster (*New York Mining Disaster*) into success nine years ago."

This was still the era of the cultural cringe, where Australians didn't think anything we created was truly worthy until someone from overseas told us it was. Hence the surprised tone that some of our bands might have some overseas success.

To capitalise on the success of *Howzat* in the UK – where they sold around a quarter of a million copies – Sherbet headed over for a seven-week tour. A tour which was much longer than their UK jaunt earlier the same year. That visit was just three warm-up dates ahead of a headlining London show.

The shows on that second tour went well according to *The Bulletin*. There could be the possibility of a little lily-gilding given it was a six-page cover story so the tour needed to be seen in as positive light as possible. But, as the band's various live albums show (and there are three of them, which is really more than a band needs) Sherbet could really pull off a great show.

Reaching the top spot on both the Australian album and singles chart is no mean feat. But it's much, much harder to stay there. For Sherbet, the highs of *Howzat* were actually the beginnings of a slow decline. The follow-up double A-side single of *Gimme Love* and *Hollywood Dreaming* stalled at No43 and, despite the big hit of *Howzat*, Porter was feeling the pressure of finding time and space to write songs.

With the band's near-constant touring schedule, the bulk of the songs for each new album were written just a few week before recording began.

"We had to do everything in such a rush that we never got to listen to new influences or experiment or anything like that," Porter said years later. "As a band we were very proud of our musicianship, but in terms of musical creativity it was a case of throwing it at the wall because we just had to get it done in time."

The release of the band's second greatest hits package slowed the decline of Sherbet a little. The album went to No5 and the re-released single *You've Got the Gun* hit No6. But it was papering over the cracks a little bit. Released in time for Christmas, sales were likely bolstered by parents buying it as a gift for their kids. And greatest hit albums are made up of songs that have already proved their worth, so it would have been more of a concern if the album tanked. Oddly for a release called *The Sherbet Collection*, it included several of Braithwaite's solo releases.

9

That songwriting struggle bit hard on Sherbet's next album *Photoplay*. When you've had a big international hit, the pressure is on to follow that up with another one. But Porter was feeling burned out. "That one felt a bit tougher because we'd had the big success in the UK and all around the world with *Howzat*," Porter told Kruger. "But we didn't quite come to grips with it. We'd been over there, we'd been touring, we'd just come back, we need a new album … Jesus."

What he wanted to do – but couldn't – was tell manager Roger Davies he was taking six months off to recharge and find some new inspiration. The result was another patchy album, where standout tracks were bolstered by filler. Among the better tracks was *High Rollin'*, written for buddy movie of the same name starring US actor Joseph Bottoms (it was a time in Australian film when the industry didn't think itself worthy, so they cast US actors in films) and marked the screen debut of Judy Davis.

The film didn't set the screen on fire. Reviewer David Stratton found it "strangely unsatisfactory, even on the most basic entertainment level; it was one of the weakest non-endings imaginable".

Despite it being one of the better tracks on the album, the record buying public didn't warm to it when it was released as the second single. It climbed no higher than No33 on the charts, which was a bit of a comedown after first single *Magazine Madonna* went to No2.

Little Darling

While the first single's lyrics speak of a cover girl model, the song was really about the experiences of being in Sherbet. "It was about us, actually," Porter said. "What happens when you get a bit older. It was autobiographical. I felt that the whole business was really disposable."

The cover played on the band's fame with the ladies. It featured a lingerie-clad woman lying on silk bed sheets with what is meant to be a sultry look in her eyes – when really, she just looks stoned. She's reading a magazine that has Sherbet on the cover, and they've decided to go back to the shirts-off look

The album also marked the start of a real push to make it the US. The *Photoplay* album was released over there as *Magazine*, which was reportedly the original title before Australian execs had the strange concern people might mistake it for an album called *Sherbet* by UK punk act Magazine – an enormously unlikely occurrence. Judging by the album art – where the woman is holding a magazine – it's likely the title change happened very late in the piece.

While the Australian audiences still liked Sherbet enough to push *Photoplay* to No4 in the charts and awarding it Australian album of the year in the *TV Week* King of Pop awards (though you have to wonder if hardcore Sherbet fans spent hours filling in multiple voting coupons to get that result), there wasn't much interest from the States. Neither the album or the single charted. Soon after the US label would decide a change had to happen if they were to crack the lucrative American market.

It's an expectation in the music scene that any band who has a largely teenage fanbase can't be that much chop onstage. There is the idea that a pop band that successful must have been manufactured and their musical success is more down to studio trickery than any actual ability to play. That's an image that has perhaps dogged Sherbet for years; this idea that they were a lightweight band who didn't have – or need – much musical ability. The crowd is full of screaming teens who cared more about what the band looked like than how they played, right?

That wasn't the case with Sherbet; they were a hard gigging band, playing plenty of shows before and after they broke through. Among those was the 'Around Australia in 80 Days' tour in support of *Photoplay*, where they played as many as 70 shows. It is still believed to be the longest Australian tour ever undertaken.

RAM's Anthony O'Grady covered part of that tour, which at times sounded like out-takes of *A Hard Day's Night* with girls following the band everywhere. O'Grady relates one instance where Porter is at a radio station in Dubbo plugging a show.

"Meantime, a mob of girls outside have found an unguarded side door and poured down the stairs where their momentum is halted by a double-glazed studio window. The horde presses against the window in an ever-expanding mass and they seem not at all overawed at being so close to two gold and platinum-certified pop stars – they exude the joy of boisterous hunters celebrating caged prey."

O'Grady's piece also captures the touring nature of the various band members. Mitchell and James are the party boys, always keen on a good time. Sandow is a stickler for being on time, while Braithwaite is perpetually late. O'Grady watches as the band is supposed to meet at 8.45am to leave on the tour bus at 9am. Obviously Sandow is the only one there on time, while Braithwaite sleeps in, has a leisurely breakfast and then waits for the taxi management will surely send him when he is required.

"Listen you lazy bastard," Sandow yells down the phone at his singer, "are you coming on this fucking tour or aren't you? Get your lazy arse into a bloody taxi and get here!"

When the singer does finally arrive, it's with a "sorry" and a shrug of the shoulders.

Apparently, the rumour is that Braithwaite does it solely to get under Sandow's skin.

Watching the band perform a show on the tour, O'Grady notes the skills of each member in turn, but saves most of his praise for Sandow.

"He's a strong man and, in concert, there's always a roadie on hand for that inevitable moment when he bends tempered steel bass drum pedals out of shape, simply by stomping them so hard. Most drummers put small dents in drumskins, Alan Sandow hits his drums so hard they crater and split. He rides his drum kit like he rides his road hog, wrestling the power."

It sounds as though he should be playing in a harder rocking band than Sherbet. Along for the ride on that tour was support band The Ted Mulry Gang. TMG drummer Herm Kovac remembered overhearing some hellish arguments going on next door in Sherbet's band room. Tensions were so high within the band, that manager Roger Davies made the decision to separate the members as much as possible to ensure the tour continued. So various TMG members would share a room with someone from Sherbet for the whole tour – except for Sandow, who got his own room.

Perhaps unwisely, given the apparent animosity between Sherbet members, Kovac got the band hooked on weaponry during that tour. Always fascinated with archery, he bought himself a bow and arrow to while away the boredom of the tour. Soon enough James, Porter and Mitchell bought bows as well and chipped in to buy a canvas-covered bulls-eye target that they carried around on the bus, dragging it off here and there for a spot of archery – with bets on who would get closest to the bulls-eye.

They moved up to pig-hunting, which led Ted Mulry and Sandow to go buy pump-action rifles – all of which made for rather unusual cargo for a touring band.

Kovac also helped Braithwaite with the distinctly un-rock and roll task of stealing tea bags from a hotel. Seems this hotel in Albury had a rare brand of tea that was cherished by Braithwaite. Rather than just ask for a stash, Braithwaite resolved to nick some. So the afternoon of the gig, Kovac found Braithwaite casing the joint, having found where the tea bag stash was hidden.

After that night's gig, Braithwaite wrangled Kovac to help him sneak into the storeroom and grab the bags. Braithwaite had even brought along a cigarette lighter he'd purchased earlier so as to avoid having to turn on any lights. The pair filled their pockets full of teabags and then headed to their room.

In late 1977 the band released a live album from that tour, *Caught In The Act … Live*. It was their fourth release in a little over a year; with the benefit of hindsight it looked as though someone was trying to milk a cash cow before time ran out. What the live album shows is an incredibly tight band; every word, every note is exactly where it should be. The band is so tight, it sounds eerie in some places. For instance, when

Porter sings *Hollywood Dreaming* it's hard to shake the feeling that they've just slipped in the studio version and added a few teenage squeals from a crowd at the end. They were *that* good.

That said, the material they chose to include on the live album is a bit … well … odd. Almost all the songs are from the band's last two albums, *Photoplay* and *Howzat*; their earlier top 10 hits like *Cassandra*, *Silvery Moon*, *Slipstream* and *Summer Love* are strangely absent. More unusual is that two of the 10 songs on the live album are covers – *You Keep Me Hangin' On* and *Nowhere Man*. Even stranger still, they released that Beatles cover as a single – which struggled to No40 on the charts. The live album didn't fare much better, reaching No33. It seemed the end was fast approaching.

10

If you want to have any chance of longevity as a band make sure the core of your fanbase isn't between the ages of 13 and 19. Fewer things will foretell of the end of your career more accurately than being a band the teens love.

It's great when they're in the early teens because they're fiercely loyal and are likely to buy any sort of crap that has your band's name on it. But then, as they move out of their teens, any music they loved then is deemed childish and pushed far, far away.

And those just entered their teenage years, well, they don't want to have their older siblings' musical hand-me-downs. They want to find their own teen idols to chew up and spit out. Sherbet started their climb to fame in 1972 and had tanked by 1979 – that's a period of eight years. That almost perfectly overlaps with the number of teenage years – seven. So Sherbet's time in the limelight was almost exactly as long as a person's teenage years.

If there is an upside to being a teen band, it's that the end really isn't a surprise. You can see if coming. "It wasn't taken away at its highest point," Porter said of Sherbet's fame. "The band soldiered on for some pretty lean years afterwards. It was a ride back down the rollercoaster as opposed to being dropped from a vertical height."

This is where the band was in 1978; the band was on the wane in Australia as their audience grew up and left behind the things of their childhood. There was still the outside chance of breaking into the US. Their American label felt the soft name of the band might have hurt their chances, so it was changed to Highway.

"Around '78 we went to Canada and did a bit of touring through there," Braithwaite told Gavin Wood. "I got a call from RSO records to come to LA because they wanted to record us but we had to consider changing the name of the band from Sherbet to something else. We left it virtually up to them and they come up with Highway."

That album was called *Highway 1* in the US, but *Sherbet* in Australia. The back cover of the Australian release, showing the four members dressed up in the "smart casual" look running towards the camera, was the front cover for the *Highway 1* album.

It was a choice of cover image that matched the sound of the band inside. Sherbet had moved away from the teenage sound of earlier albums and very much towards "adult contemporary". It had a very 'American' sound (the yacht-rock sax intro to *Skyline* is just one example of that), which is something Braithwaite said the band noticed at the time. He said the band was happier with the demoes they'd recorded than with the finished product which "ended up sounding like LA".

The album contained a strong hint the band was running on empty; at least creatively speaking. The album included a tune from the dreaded "life on the road" genre of musical cliches. So many bands do it a few albums into their careers; it happens when they're always on a tour bus going from one show to the next and have no chance to draw on outside sources for inspiration. And so they write about being on a tour bus going from one show to the next.

That's how it was for Sherbet and the first single from the album *Another Night on the Road*. "We were travelling all around the world," Porter told Debbie Kruger. "We were touring or we were recording. That was it. And so it's a song about the boring side or the monotony, the routine the continuity of it all. At that time I would have had nothing else in my head that registered."

That song just made it to No10 on the charts – which would end up being the band's last 10 top 10 song. The other single from the band was one of their best tunes. *(Feels Like It's) Slipping Away* unfairly stalled at No22 when it deserved much better. And of course, the song title became something used to mock the band; they said it referred to Sherbet's career trajectory. Another cracker was *Winnipeg Sidestep*, which pointed at a possible way forward for the band. It was a more grown-up sound, and was one of the few songs on the album not to be stripped of all feeling by the sheen of the US production.

The third and final single from the album – *Beg, Steal or Borrow* – wasn't even noticed by the charts. Which is really what it deserved. In 1979, Sherbet put out two singles. The first was *Angela*, a track written for the Australian thriller *Snapshot*. The song reached a distant No85 on the charts. After that release, the band ditched the name Sherbet and adopted Highway, the one created for them by their US label.

In August 1979, they released yet another greatest hits collection (oddly under the name of Sherbet). The collection included a new tune called *Heart Get Ready* – which was released under the name Highway to totally confuse everybody. It was a more grown-up pop sound, but it came a little too late. It did even worse than *Angela*, reaching No89 on the charts.

When nothing really happened in the States either, the band quietly pulled the pin. Thus Sherbet was no more.

Little Darling

11

With Sherbet gone, Braithwaite decided to give his solo career another go. He didn't muck around either – *Out On The Fringe* came out in 1979, the same year Sherbet called it quits. If you weren't aware of this solo album from Braithwaite, there is a reason for that. It really isn't very good, despite some reviewers trying to big it up by outlandishly claiming "it's a knockout!"

Perhaps looking to stand on his own two feet, he chose to ignore Sherbet's established songwriting talent of Garth Porter and Tony Mitchell. Instead he went with two guys named Terry Shaddick and Bruce Donnelly. Shaddick was a few years away from his claim to fame – co-writing *Physical* for Braithwaite's old school chum Olivia Newton-John, and there was nothing on *Out on the Fringe* that sounded anything like that. Or anything like a hit either.

The production feels lifeless, the songs feel lifeless; even Braithwaite's own performance sounds underwhelming, like he's realised this whole thing with US session musos was a mistake but he just has to soldier on. As evidence of that, *Out on the Fringe* has fallen through the cracks; it's not available on Braithwaite's Spotify channel and just one song from the album – *Love Like a Child* – appears on any of his best-of albums (and he's released at least four of those).

With Braithwaite's first post-Sherbet release not even coming close to doing the business, it was lucky the old band came to his rescue. The break-up didn't last long; in 1980 they were back as The Sherbs, boasting a tougher new wave sound and a new album in *The Skill*. The aim was to reinvent the band, but the local audience were having none of it. That's the problem with being teenage heart-throbs; your audience grows up and moves onto more "mature" things, while their younger siblings want to find their own band, rather than taking their older sister's hand-me-downs.

And those who didn't like Sherbet, well, they weren't going to have any interest in this new version. The choice of band name didn't help distance the band from their 1970s selves. It was like they were having a bet each way; becoming a "new" band while still wanting the name recognition of their past.

All of which is a pity, really, because it was as The Sherbs that the band did some of their best stuff. It's shorter, sharper and much more direct – all when no-one here was paying attention.

Ironically, *The Skill* was finally an album where the US decided to pay attention. The album reached No100 on the Billboard top 100 albums chart – the first time any of their albums charted in America. The single *I Have the Skill* reached No14 on the Billboard Rock Tracks chart.

But for some dumb reason, the band was plugging away in Australia to uninterested punters rather than striking out for the US.

"*The Skill* immediately got an American deal," Porter told Debbie Kruger. "But we never went to America and toured it over there. I don't know why. So while this great news was happening to us in America we were playing to 20 and 30 people on door deals here."

From this point on, it was a case of diminishing returns; the second Sherbs album *Defying Gravity* didn't do much on the charts, neither did the seven-track mini album *Shaping Up*. The band could see the writing on the wall; The Sherbs were no more, and Sherbet returned for a farewell tour. And that was it.

Though there would be a footnote years later. In 2013 French dance duo Daft Punk would sample The Sherbs' *We Ride Tonight* from *Defying Gravity* on its track *Contact*. Thomas Bangalter – who is one of the people under those helmets – had previously used the Sherbs track to close out his DJ sets

"It was out of the blue and now it looks like Daft Punk is going to be one of the big releases of the year," Braithwaite said.

"You feel thrilled about it and I'm sure Garth, Tony and Alan who were co-writers will feel really good about it too."

12

With Sherbet/The Sherbs now officially done with (barring the occasional reformation down the line caused by the nostalgia-fuelled 21st century), Braithwaite had to find some other way to earn a crust. Despite the popularity of Sherbet, Braithwaite hadn't ended up financially secure. "We probably could have made a lot more money but we spent a lot," he said. "We always wanted to do things bigger and better than anyone else – bigger trucks, better motels."

Singing was the obvious choice to earn a few quid but he decided he didn't want to do that. So he went on the dole, and soon the people in the office found him a job on a road gang with the council.

"I was quite nervous fronting up to Bulla Shire Council and saying 'Hi, I'm Daryl Braithwaite, I'm meant to report here and go to work'," Braithwaite said. "I can remember the guy looking up at me and going 'right, okay'."

Understandably, his co-workers were confused as well; we're here because we have to be – we can't find a job, they'd say. But you, you were famous, what are you doing here?

"I was on the dole," he said. "I didn't want to do club singing. Not so much [because it's] boring. Not degrading either. But I just thought, 'that's prostitution'."

The guys felt Braithwaite was wasting his time on a shovel with them. They felt he should be singing, but not the old Sherbet stuff – some new songs. Coincidentally, it had been the same thing Braithwaite's then wife Sarah had been telling him for a while now.

So he took the shot and headed to Sydney on weekends to work on songs that would become the *Edge* album. The timing was handy. In the 1980s John Farnham's career was in a place not too dissimilar to Braithwaite's. He'd joined the Little River Band just after they'd had their career highpoint and, by the mid-1980s it looked as though Farnham's best days were in the rear-view mirror.

Then, in late 1986, he released an album called *Whispering Jack*, and suddenly everyone wanted a piece of Farnham. The damned thing went platinum 24 times over, became the highest selling album in Australia by a Australian artist and spawned the No1 single *You're The Voice*. Oh, and the album went to No1 too.

So if you were an old singer – Braithwaite would be nudging 40 when *Edge* was released – hoping for a career resurgence, Farnham had just shown it was entirely possible.

"I think he opened a door that had been firmly shut for a while," Braithwaite said. "After Farnham, the record companies were more willing to give people like me a chance."

But that didn't mean labels were lining up to sign the former Sherbet frontman. Farnham's success had shown older performers could still crank out big hits, but Braithwaite still had to convince others that it could be him that could do it.

"The record companies didn't seem to take me seriously," Braithwaite said. "I first tried the company that had had Sherbet. They would have signed me as a favour, but I didn't want that. I wanted to prove that I could make a really good album."

Edge came out in November 1988, but the initial response from the public was lukewarm. "I think people had this preconceived idea of what Daryl Braithwaite was," he said. "They thought 'oh no, that guy out of Sherbet'.

"The record was going nowhere and I thought, that's it, but after three singles people seemed to realise that maybe it wasn't so bad after all."

Around six months after *Edge* was released, it finally reached No1 on the charts and towards the end of 1989 had sold more than 250,000 copies. It went triple platinum, and spawned five singles – *As the Days Go By*, *All I Do*, *One Summer*, *Let Me Be* and *Sugar Train*. Only *One Summer* would crack the top 10.

The success of the album was handy for Braithwaite. Not only did it prove he still had the ability to sell records, the fact he had fronted up the cost of the recording meant he would have gotten more money coming his way from those sales.

Little Darling

13

And so here we are. It's 1990 and Braithwaite is working on his follow-up to *Edge*, that will also go by a one-word title, *Rise*. He's got 11 songs in the bag for the album, which is enough for most performers. In what would become a stroke of good fortune for Braithwaite, he figures he needs one more tune. Who knows why, maybe he's got a thing against odd numbers. One story is that a friend gave him a hot tip.

"We were near the end of recording it and

a friend of mine, I think he mentioned to is to me, if you've got the Rickie Lee Jones album *Flying Cowboys* have a listen to it," Braithwaite said on Steve Bell's *Rewind* podcast.

"I remember going home after being in the studio. I got the CD out put it on and the first track was *The Horses* and I thought 'My God, how good is that?' as soon as I heard it."

Braithwaite wasn't hearing a single; for him *The Horses* would be an album track. He figured producer Simon Hussey could make it into something in the vein of *As The Days Go By* from *Edge*.

For his part Hussey wasn't so sure when Braithwaite played him the song in his blue Mazda 323. The female vocalist put him off; when they were fishing around for songs for Braithwaite, they always went with male singer-songwriters. Also, the way Hussey remembered it, they already had enough songs for the album; he wouldn't have gone into the studio with anything less. At the time Braithwaite found *The Horses*, they'd already called in session player John Watson to record all the drums – you don't do that unless you've already got all the songs finished.

"I remember hearing this and thinking 'it's just too soulful' and that it didn't sound like Daryl at all to me," Hussey told Bell. "I thought 'how are we going to make this a Daryl song?'"

What he did included adding the intro with that marimba-like sound (neither of which appear on the Jones original), scrapped the breakdown and made it into the traditional verse-chorus-verse format with a fade-out where Jones' version just noodles its way to the end of the song. "My role as producer and arranger was that I'd get the scissors out, making the songs more succinct," Hussey told journalist Cameron Adams. "*The Horses* in particular needed some editing."

It didn't need much work in terms of Braithwaite's vocal delivery. Hussey remembers the singer nailing it in one take. And until the mixing stage, his were the only vocals that appeared on the track (music geeks should note that both John Farnham and Skyhooks' Graham "Shirley" Strachan sang backing vocals for other tracks on *Rise*).

Hussey figured *The Horses* needed some sort of vocal accompaniment for Braithwaite. His wife Elizabeth suggested New Zealand singer Margaret Urlich, who had released her debut *Safety in Numbers* the year before and picked up an ARIA.

"We'd never used a female vocalist with Daryl before," Hussey said. "Being on the same label, she was in the county. We got in touch with her and she said yes. We sent her a version and she listened to the original as well and agreed to do it."

Urlich went in and recorded her bit while listening to Braithwaite's lines through headphones (he was in China visiting a friend at the time). "I didn't really think much of it at all after that, except Daryl did an incredible vocal and it was a cool song,"

Urlich said.

It got to the stage where Hussey thought Urlich's backing vocals sounded so good, he cut Braithwaite's vocals out at a few points, making it somewhat more of a duet. And so they put it as track eight on the album.

14

There was no way *The Horses* would be the first release from *Rise*. In the music world, you don't rush out of the gates with the ballad (unless you're, say, Air Supply, and your whole schtick is ballads), Instead, in November 1990, they went with the title track.

It would be the second year in a row *Rise* was released as a single. It was written by Sydney band The Chosen Few, who released it as a single in 1989 – which sounded more folky and less poppy than Braithwaite's version. That may be partly why The Chosen Few only got to No120 with their version, while Braithwaite got to No23. Any jealousy the songwriters felt was probably tempered by the extra royalties they raked in from Braithwaite's version.

The Horses was let out of the gate in January 1991. "The record company did see something in it once everything was done," Hussey said. "They obviously saw the catchiness in it but when we were making it even Daryl didn't think there was anything that was going to blow the world away."

At first it seemed Braithwaite might have been right. Just after it was released *The Horses* didn't do a whole lot. It didn't crack the top 100 until February 10, when it snuck in at No99. But then, rather than disappearing, *The Horses* kept on hanging around. By April it had made its way into the top 10, and slowly made its way along until it got to the No1 spot in May, where it stayed for two weeks.

It would spend 23 weeks in the top 50, 30 in the top 100, become the fifth highest-selling song that year and help take *Rise* to No3 on the album charts and go four times platinum, selling 300,000 copies.

To help push *The Horses* up the charts, the record label sent Braithwaite to a beach at Sandbar, on the NSW North Coast to shoot a video. Shot by Grant Matthews, he told Cameron Adams the idea was to move him away from the teeny Sherbet image into something more sophisticated. "That was part of it, even the wardrobe," he said. "Everything was designed to make him little more fashionable and a little less rock and roll.. It's such an emotional song, I didn't want the visuals to distract from the music."

In terms of the wardrobe, all Braithwaite remembers is that blue jumper tucked into his pants.

The budget for the video was around $45,000, some of which went to the poor guy who spent six hours in the middle of the night sweeping the beach with a broom.

"When you're doing overhead shots you don't want car tracks on the beach," Matthews explained. Turned out the guy wasted his time – after he'd finished with the broom a huge storm rose up and would have swept the beach clean anyway.

The interesting thing about the clip is that it features model Gillian Bailey lip-synching Urlich's lines. Urlich was in London working on her album at the time of the shot and didn't want the distraction of heading back for a day.

"If I hadn't already had a successful album and I was still up and coming I would have probably rushed home to be in the video," Urlich said. "Nothing against Daryl at all, he's a lovely guy, but at the time I felt I was so focused on my own album.

"In retrospect it was probably a little but silly because the song was so huge. But at the time I was young and a bit stupid. I did what I thought was right."

Rather than get another singer in to do the video – they'd be criticised for singing someone else's part – model Gillian Bailey was drafted in for the job.

"I got the lyrics the night before the shoot and I had to learn them quickly," she told Adams. "I listened to the song on my Walkman while driving to the shoot in my old bomb of a car. I was really nervous. Miming was the really scary part. I was nicknamed Gilli Vanilli for a while!"

Later that night, after the filming was finished, Braithwaite headed straight to St George Leagues Club for a gig. With a sunburnt face – he'd forgotten to wear any sunscreen during the shoot.

Around this time Braithwaite had a chance to break into the US market, with former Sherbet manager Roger Davies now a heavy hitter in the American market. The US label released an album that took songs from *Edge* and *Rise*. The first single, *Higher Than Hope* (a Braithwaite co-write with Hussey) went to No47 on the US charts. While that seems a credible result for a newcomer to the US market, it wasn't good enough for the Americans who went cold on Braithwaite after that.

15

Critics may look down their noses at *The Horses*, suggesting its popularity is a case of, as someone once said, you'll never go broke under-estimating the taste of the public. But really, who cares what music critics say any more? Really, we're long past the stage where we need some self-appointed cabal of musical deep thinkers to tell us plebs what we should listen to and what we should avoid like the plague.

When you can get almost any song you

want to hear in seconds, do we really need rock critics to help us filter through the stream of new releases by telling what's cool and what's not? (well, not that critics tell the truth these days – who wants to criticise an album by a popular artist these days and risk the inevitable online onslaught from fans?). Maybe back in the day they had some value, when you had to reach into your pocket for money to buy an album, cassette or CD if you wanted to listen to some new music. In that bygone age, you searched out some degree of assurance that a record you were considering might be alright. That it was cool, that you weren't going to burn with anger towards the album when you realised it was utter crap and you'd wasted around $20 to $30.

Today you don't need to ask a rock critic what they think before you buy. You can hear it for yourself. A band puts a new album out and you go straight to a certain streaming service (which you may not have even paid for) to check it out in its entirety

– not just the singles, even the deep cuts. And then, if it passes muster, you might go out and buy it. But you probably won't, because as this exercise just illustrated, you can hear the album without walking out the door with your wallet.

No wonder bands are having a hard time making a buck these days. Those micro-royalties from streaming really don't add up to much. Really, that's why you should actually buy a physical copy of albums you like – as a show of support to the artist who created them.

In fact, it'd be that very streaming service that is in part responsible for the continued popularity of *The Horses*. It wasn't the spark that lit the fire, but it was certainly the winds that fanned the spark into a blaze, to extend a crappy metaphor.

At the time of writing, *The Horses* is easily Braithwaite's most downloaded song; it's been listened to more than 61 million times. From there it's a whole lot of daylight to his second-most popular, the *One Summer* single from the *Edge* album with a comparatively paltry 21 million spins.

Those 61 million listens are evidence that the phenomenon of *The Horses* doesn't rely solely on going to see Braithwaite perform it live (though he probably has performed it roughly 61 million times since it was released). Maybe people read a story about *The Horses* being this millennial thing and it leads to them searching for it on Spotify. Maybe it's the millennials themselves who were part of a drunk singalong at a recent Braithwaite show who go back and listen to it at home to relieve a few fond memories.

Whatever the reason, the streaming option allows people to fill in the gaps between Daryl Braithwaite tours. It allows them to play it at parties, when friends are over for dinner, at family events, when they're riding the train to work – wherever they listen to music. Every time they do it just reinforces their connection to the song. And every time they play it to others, it allows the song's popularity to spread.

And, as we've already established, hardly anyone actually buys music any more. So the suggestion that the youngsters propelling the song forward might actually own any vinyl with *The Horses* on it is laughable. They're all streaming it – what we're seeing with *The Horses* just wouldn't have happened any other way.

16

Just when things were going well for Braithwaite, the Fates decided to give him a big kick in the teeth. In mid-1992, he was sued by a pair of men with rhyming surnames, Simon Fenner and Nathan Brenner. In the Victorian Supreme Court case, they alleged they managed Braithwaite from 1987 to 1988 before being sacked when the first single from *Edge* was released. Claiming they weren't paid, the pair asked for a $600,000 payout. Braithwaite said he was managed by First Artists Management and that Fenner and Brenner, who worked for the company, were not his managers.

In court, Brenner's QC claimed his client and Fenner were responsible for Braithwaite's success. The singer disagreed, to put it mildly. "It is a big statement," he said in court. "No, I think it is highly exaggerated to the point of bullshit." Instead, he credited his then wife Sarah with the career rejuvenation in late 1988, pointing out that in 1987, after giving up the cabaret-style performances at the nation's RSL clubs, he was so hard up for money, he had to go on the dole. For that year he had a taxable income of a whopping $475. He and Sarah had so much owing on their home in Mt Macedon, outside Melbourne that they had to sell and move into something smaller in Carlton.

In the end, Braithwaite had to pay the pair, though the judge awarded them far less than the $600,000 they were after. Braithwaite had to pull out $35,000 from his bank account to pay the pair. "It has been a strain in more ways than one, but some people have been very supportive, like out here on the street," Braithwaite said outside the court. "You walk along to court during those seven weeks and people would be very comforting in what they said, but I hope I never go through it again."

Braithwaite would later have to pay an estimated $500,000 in court costs, which would have chewed up a sizeable amount of the money he'd made from *Edge* and *Rise*. He basically had to start all over again; he even ended up accepting fellow musicians' offer of a charity concert to help him out.

"You have to weigh up whether to take charity or not. I call it charity no matter how anyone phrases it," he said. "I do like to fight my own way out of battles. I thought about it for a week. I looked at all the alternatives and there weren't many except the possibility of going bankrupt.

"I nearly cancelled [but] I just decided I was accepting it for the right reason – my friends wanted to help and I needed help."

Years later, Braithwaite would explain he was still friends with one of the pair who were suing him (he didn't specify which).

"We sometimes talk about it and even though we were on opposing sides, it was all a big waste of time, money and effort," Braithwaite said. "It was what they call a pyrrhic victory – it cost them so much and they only got $10,000 out of it, yet about $500,000 went into the legal fraternity."

His first recording after that big setback was as a singer for Hussey's project Company of Strangers. "This project grew out of my frustration with producing all the time," Hussey said. "All that creative energy was going into arranging other people's songs and it was taking away from my writing."

Having worked with Braithwaite on his last two albums, and Australian Crawl's James Reyne during both that band's last album and the singer's solo projects, Hussey managed to convince the pair to lend their vocals to his new project.

"Company of Strangers is a celebration of my involvement with those guys," Hussey said.

"The records have been very successful and I feel lucky to have been a part of it. But if that's the last time I work with them this is a great way to go out: with something we just came together and did for the fun of it."

The album went to No9 with *The Age* calling it "high-tech, high-sheen, hook-laden, cleverly conceived pop". Of the four singles spun off it, the highest placing was No21. There were a few ARIA nominations for the group, with Hussey winning Producer of the Year, perhaps an irony given the whole idea of the band was to move away from behind the recording desk.

17

Much to his dismay, Braithwaite hasn't been big on songwriting. He had a hand in just three of the 14 songs on *Edge* (though one was a solo credit for the hit *One Summer*) and just two on *Rise*. As well as the creative satisfaction, there are also the potentially lucrative royalties that flow to the songwriter. That's why, when it comes to *The Horses*, Ricki Lee Jones likely gets more money from Braithwaite's version than he does.

"If I have one regret, it's that I'm not a songwriter," Braithwaite said. "I have written songs occasionally but not enough and that's because of laziness and lack of application."

It was the same story with the 1993 release *Taste The Salt* (which could be a reference to the ocean or to the tears shed during his recent stressful court case). Braithwaite's name appeared in the writing credits for just three of the tunes.

"On *Taste the Salt*, I've written probably about the same as on *Edge* and *Rise*, about 25 per cent," he said when the album was released.

"I guess that's the only thing that disappoints me. Someone said to me yesterday that I'd found songs that maybe I would have liked to have written and when you sing them you make them your own anyway.

"But I said to them 'yeah, that's all well and good' but at the end of the day you'd like to feel that you're accomplished, you'd like to give the whole lot, so that interviewers don't say 'so you've written two songs on this album' and you go into defensive mode. That's one of the drawbacks, that I haven't made that achievement."

At the time the album was released, the 43-year-old started to feel like he was taking up space that might be better used by an 18-year-old musician waiting for their go. "And then I thought, 'no hang on, don't be too savage on yourself because what you've done is you've pulled away from the Sherbet thing, you're doing your own songs and it's new to you'."

In that same interview, Braithwaite bemoaned trying to make a living in music without "selling your soul and doing all the things you hear people do now, like in-store appearances or with every album you get a free trip and [competitions] to meet [artists] and you get to play in their back yard?"

"What's it got to? I'd rather not play the game. I'd rather get out of it."

Little Darling

Those words turned out to be oddly prophetic. *Taste The Salt* didn't perform as well as the last two albums. It reached No13 and first single *The World As It Is* reached No35, with follow-up *Barren Ground* getting no higher than No61.

As a result, Sony dropped Braithwaite, with the obligatory mining of the back catalogue for greatest hits collection *Six Moons* being his last release with the label.

From there Braithwaite had a short stint as a TV host with *Dreams Can Come True* in 1996 and another short stint in *Chess the Musical* the following year. In 1999 he turned 50 and his career was definitely in another one of those troughs.

He was still plugging away on the touring circuit but with no record company, there was no new album to plug. In fact, it would take Braithwaite more than 10 years to release his next album – 2005's self-released *Snapshot*.

"I think I got lazy and a little bit of cold feet," Braithwaite said of the decade-long wait. "Because I'm not with a record company there's this sense of apprehension – 'will it work or won't it'? I'm now at the point where I think 'bugger it, I'll just do it'. You make an album, initially, to please yourself and you hope other people like it."

It's hard to say whether other people liked it – because so few of them actually heard it. Without the label muscle behind it, *Snapshot* quickly fell through the cracks.

"I put out an album independently and realised then how hard and important promotion is," he said. "You realise that the $100,000 [record labels] allocate to promotion is a necessity. You put out an album thinking people will know, but of course they don't and no-one buys it. It was a learning curve. But, if you were bitter and twisted then you wouldn't want to be in this industry."

It was disappointing for Braithwaite but there was good news on the horizon – the horses were about to bolt.

18

There's a handy online tool called Google Trends, which allows you to see what people had been searching for over the years. Stretch out the timeline and you can see the peaks and troughs of the trends. So if you enter the search terms "Daryl Braithwaite" and "The Horses" the resulting line graph you get back shows two big spikes in 2004, one late in the year. That's a time that coincides with various comments from Braithwaite in the 2000s, when journalists started asking him what the hell was going on with *The Horses*?

"We first started to notice it four years ago in Perth," he told the *Cairns Post* in 2009. "We did this gig and the first 100 people down the front were all aged between 18 and 25 and we thought 'God, what's going on?'. They sang all of the songs off *Edge* and *Rise* and when we played *The Horses* the whole place erupted."

Comments made to other journalists also point back to the time around 2004 as being the moment something started happening with *The Horses*. As to just what that inspiration was isn't clear. It might be a job for another music historian to go back and see what was going on.

From there the popularity of *The Horses* slowly grew, in part through the obvious synergy of getting Braithwaite to sing it in sponsors' tents at horse races. The song still hadn't reached iconic status by 2007, when Braithwaite made an appearance on *Neighbours*. Toadie's aunt Janelle was getting married and, knowing she was a huge Sherbet fan, the groom snagged Braithwaite as a surprise wedding guest. He serenaded Janelle with a rendition of *One Summer*.

The fact there was a wedding going on and the producers didn't ask Braithwaite to sing *The Horses* (now a wedding staple) strongly suggests the song hadn't reached the level it is at now.

Perhaps the moment that really led to the resurgence of *The Horses* was Braithwaite's appearance on the Hamish and Andy radio show in 2008. The pair had to compete to get Braithwaite choose them as his "Brathmate". For the record, Andy won that one.

Braithwaite has since acknowledged that as one of the tipping points for *The Horses*. And given the radio show would have been syndicated across the country, it exposed Braithwaite to a lot of younger ears.

"I think things like that exposed *The Horses* to a different audience and for it to be accepted for some reason no matter what age group and gets over the last five years or so just continues that line of thought," he said.

Another was his regular appearances in Melbourne for the Cox Plate. They went as far back as 2007, when the lyrics to *The Horses* were printed in the race booklet. The *Herald Sun* reported the song went "for about 10 minutes as the record crowd joined in chorus after chorus".

In 2008, Braithwaite was keen to return. "I have been looking forward to this performance ever since I got the call asking me to do it. The song got such a good reception last year. Even the younger people know the words. It seems to have been passed on to the next generation."

The popularity of the song caused some problems at the 2010 Cox Plate with the band still playing as the horses were being led out onto the track. Some of the nags were actually spooked by *The Horses*, which didn't sit well with Moonee Valley Racing Club CEO Michael Browell.

"No horse was injured or I would say

their performance impacted in any way as a result of it but the club's certainly not happy that the performance by Daryl Braithwaite, instead of going nine minutes – he decided to extend it out to over 12," Mr Browell said.

The incident caused a bit of controversy, with champion trainer Bart Cummings complaining "it's not a concert; it's a racetrack". Calmer heads prevailed and Braithwaite was back the following year.

Three years later and *The Horses* rode on the back of Hawthorn' three-peat as AFL Premiers from 2013-15. During that first season, *The Horses* became the team victory song, courtesy of Brent "Goo" Guerra

"We had a really stirring victory in Perth in early 2013," said coach Alistair Clarkson, " and it was Goo's favourite song, so he belted it out after the game. And it has become a little bit of a tradition for us whenever we have a really good interstate win - we get *Horses* going."

Guerra admitted he got up and sang the song at every wedding he attended and that it was a highlight that he got to sing it with Braithwaite at a season launch during the run of premierships.

By 2013, the song had become popular enough that Sony decided to re-sign the singer they ditched more than a decade ago. "Daryl is an icon of the Australian music industry and we are delighted to welcome him home to Sony Music," Sony boss Denis Handlin said in the obligatory press release.

The result was the album *Forever The Tourist*, where Braithwaite had a hand in writing six of the eight songs. It would have surely pleased the man, who had always beat himself up about not writing enough of the songs he recorded.

"It sometimes gets annoying when people say 'why don't you write?' and I say 'well, yeah I'm lazy' or whatever it is," Braithwaite said.

"During COVID I sat here and persevered day after day. My attention span may be good for an hour and then I think it's not working and I'll go outside and have a look at the garden or something.

"I don't have that perseverance I think that songwriters need to have."

By 2017, *The Horses* was well and truly a phenomenon and the continuing attention likely led to Braithwaite being inducted into the ARIA Hall of Fame as a solo performer, having already been in there since 1990 as a member of Sherbet.

"I feel very honoured to be inducted into the ARIA Hall Of Fame, in an industry that I started out in because I was so passionate about it," Braithwaite said. "I loved music, and being associated with my band members at the time. It's been a great journey and life through music, and all its associated with, especially with the public that I get to perform to."

That same year he finally performed *The Horses* with Ricki Lee Jones onstage during her Australian tour.

Braithwaite actually tried to contact Jones in the early 2000s through her manager to let her know about the ongoing success of *The*

Horses but got silence in return. Then in late 2016, they started emailing each other, which led to a duet on *The Horses* when Jones played the Melbourne Recital Centre during her 2017 tour.

They meet in person for the first time in her hotel the day before the show, where they talked about the effect *The Horses* has on people in Australia. And then she told him soundcheck was at 4.30pm.

"I would have been happy just to have met her," Braithwaite said. "I was not expecting to sing with her. She said maybe you take the second verse because I will be playing guitar and I am a bit clunky."

The performance was a bit clunky as well. Part of that was due to the fact Braithwaite's version is different from the one Jones originally recorded. His version is almost a minute shorter than hers; in fact, when you think she's winding up the tune, there's still another minute of the song to go. Also Jones' version is more low-key and less poppy than Braithwaite's – it's hard to imagine a crowd singing along with her.

On top of that, during the live performance Jones started off the song even slower than the version on the album and threw in some really odd phrasing and accents on certain words. Hell, in the online footage, she even seems to forget the words. Throughout the performance, Braithwaite looks awkward, unsure of when Jones is going to sing or even whether she'll suddenly change the tempo of the song.

Oddly enough, Jones chose not to mention Braithwaite by name in her 2021 autobiography. Nor does she mention this duet. She dedicates just a page to *The Horses* phenomenon, writing about how she was on an Australian tour in 2010 and turned on the TV. Flicking through the channels, she stopped on coverage of a horse race. "… in the middle of the stadium was a singer. He seemed familiar – and I heard a song I knew well. That was the moment I discovered that my song *The Horses* had become the unofficial Australian national anthem. The entire stadium was singing my song! It was awesome! Dude!".

By the time she wrote that, she had met Braithwaite so she could have easily called him by name. Yet she elected to make him effectively anonymous. It's an odd way to repay someone who was responsible for a not insubstantial boost in her royalties. Braithwaite's version has gone 10 times platinum in Australia, selling more than 700,000 copies. It went to No1 in Australia, while Jones' version didn't even chart. Indirectly, Braithwaite gave Jones her biggest hit since *Chuck E's in Love* all the way back in 1979.

A little recognition in her autobiography wouldn't have gone astray.

19

So, just what is it about *The Horses*, why is it still so popular? It's a question Braithwaite is no doubt sick of hearing, because he doesn't really have an answer. And, to be fair, he probably doesn't keep himself up at night wondering what the secret is because, just maybe, if he figured it out it would ruin everything.

But you've come this far, so perhaps you want some sort of answer. But at the risk of coming across as being that guy who answers a question with a question, I'll put this forward right at the start; 'why shouldn't it be popular?'. It's far from the only song from decades gone by that the youngsters have grabbed onto and still sing in groups. There are kids singing Cold Chisel's *Khe Sanh*, who weren't even born when it was released in 1978. Crowds at AC/DC shows are full of 20-somethings who know all the words to *Highway to Hell*. Hunters & Collectors' *Throw Your Arms Around Me* has long been a song for the drunken choir. And *Don't Dream It's Over* by Crowded House will get people singing, even those who weren't born when it was released.

When *Power and the Passion* is played around a bunch of 20-year-olds at a party, if they're drunk enough they'll sing along. No doubt someone will be drunk enough to do the Peter Garrett dance too.

The point here is that there are quite a few Australian songs that have crossed over into other generations. Yet, no-one asks the question 'why?' of a Midnight Oil song, a

Crowded House tune or something from the Cold Chisel canon.

But they do ask that when it comes to *The Horses*. There's an underlying snobbishness there. The subtext is 'why is it *that* song?' as though the asker feels it is somehow not worthy. The Oils, Acca Dacca or the Hunnas? Yeah, they're worthy, you don't even need to ask the question. But *The Horses*? Well, that was meant to be a throwaway pop song that should have faded away back in the 1990s. Embedded in the question 'Why *The Horses*?' is the subtext that it really shouldn't have happened – because it's such a crap song.

That sort of veiled snobbery is something Braithwaite is familiar with. He's had hits over four decades, was in a band that had 20 hit singles in 10 years and released 10 platinum albums, is in the ARIA Hall of Fame as a member of Sherbet and a solo performer and has an iconic song to his name, but still genuine respect is elusive.

In 2010 music writers John O'Donnell,

Toby Creswell and Craig Mathieson compiled a book of the 100 best Australian albums. Did Braithwaite or Sherbet get look-in? Nope. Some might mount an argument that Sherbet were a singles band not an albums band, but The Easybeats, Slim Dusty, Johnny O'Keefe, The Seekers, Russell Morris, Normie Rowe and Bee Gees made their list via greatest hits albums. Which suggests it was felt those artists *should* be on the list, even if they didn't have a studio album good enough to warrant inclusion. But a Sherbet best of? Nope.

In 2020 *Rolling Stone* published a list of the 50 greatest Australian artists of all time. Somehow newcomers like Tame Impala (No7), 5 Seconds of Summer (No16) and King Gizzard and the Lizard Wizard (No47) made it. Jesus, even Air Supply made the cut. But Braithwaite? Nope, well aside from his writing a piece about old school chum Olivia Newton-John (No20). Both Sherbet and Braithwaite appear on an "honourable mentions" list, alongside acts that have been around for five minutes.

Rolling Stone followed that up with a collection of the top 200 Australian albums. You think they could squeeze in a Sherbet or Braithwaite album in there somewhere? Nope. They found room for Tame Impala (*twice*), Wolfmother, Killing Heidi, Icehouse, Custard, The Fauves, Frente, Sticky Fingers but not for the biggest band of the 1970s. The last page features a list of "honourable mentions" numbering more than 200 albums. Guess who's not there. Because Sherbet – and therefore Braithwaite – aren't *cool*.

Value judgements are tricky in music; so often they're used more to make someone feel superior to someone else. It's the old 'my taste in music is great – what you listen to is crap' story. And then there's the idea that it has to be crap because it went to No1; the thinking goes that, if a lot of people like song, then it can't be good (unless of course a song you like goes to No1, then it's validation of your good taste).

For a song to be cool, they think, well it has to have a smaller audience of people who *know* good music. Like themselves, of course. It's an argument that obviously falls to pieces the moment something they liked gets popular; because the song itself hasn't changed, the only difference is more people like it. So clearly it was a judgement based on how cool liking the song made them feel, and the resentment that other people sharing the joy of the song robbed it of that coolness.

The Horses obviously isn't a bad song. It was written by Ricki Lee Jones, who is very much a critics' darling – largely because she hasn't had any hits and so liking her still means those critics can feel 'cool'. How can someone both respect the songwriter but hate the song they wrote?

Listening to Jones' and Braithwaite's versions side by side, it's undeniable that the latter is better. His version breathes life into what sounded like an album filler from Jones. Braithwaite sings the hell out of it; it's a fine vocal effort. And while the chorus comes with a traditional uplift, Braithwaite goes against expectations and sings that part straight. It's during the more delicate verses that he boosts his vocal range. But it's far from Mariah Carey-style vocal gymnastics, he manages to stay within the song, rather than making himself bigger than it.

It's something Jones herself admitted, the song was so popular because he sung it better than she did.

But there are reasons why the song became successful and has reached out to a new audience. Theoretically, it's something that could happen to any song but the confluence of events that gave us the phenomenon of *The Horses* are pretty hard to replicate. In fact, as one of the steps show, trying to *make* it happen won't work.

So, here's my theory to explain the popularity of *The Horses*.

This has nothing to do with it

Sorry to start off with something that

doesn't explain the popularity of *The Horses*, but it's important to get this out of the way right at the start.

One theory that has been put forward a number of times to explain the popularity of *The Horses* is nostalgia. Basically, the kids listening to the song now had parents who liked the song and played it heaps. So, the theory claims, *The Horses* gives those kids a huge shot of nostalgia for their childhood and that's why they like it.

There are a few problems with that theory. The first is the age gap. For that to happen, it would mean the kids' parents still had *The Horses* on high rotation at home a decade after the song was released. Maybe a few grown-ups were listening to that song 10 years later, but no way would there have been enough of them to explain this trend. And just because your mate's mum loved *The Horses* doesn't mean you're going to like it.

Secondly, if that's all it took for a song to cross generations – why doesn't it happen all the time? The very reason people are interested in *The Horses* is because it's unusual for a song to jump from one generation to another.

Yet if all it took for teens and 20-somethings to form a strong attachment to a song was parents playing it around the house heaps when they were little then there would be plenty of songs that have done what *The Horses* did. There were plenty of other songs from the early 1990s that shifted more units than *The Horses*, but we're not seeing kids singing them in pubs.

No 20-something gets all wistful when they hear Bryan Adams' *Everything I Do* played over the bar's sound system. No-one gets excited to hear *Do The Bartman*, *Read My Lips* or *More Than Words* – all of which were hits in the year of *The Horses*.

Finally, when do kids *ever* like the music their parents play? How many adults can say they love a certain song because their parents listened to it heaps? If you're seven years old and your dad keeps playing *The*

Horses you're going to be sick of it and want him to play something you like. So when you're older and hear the song played, it's going to remind you of those negative memories, which is hardly going to inspire fondness for the song.

So, if that didn't lead to the popularity of the song, then what did?

The song

Obviously the quality and content of the song itself is crucial. People don't have a tendency to take crap songs into their heart – well, not for the length of time they do with *The Horses*. Producer Hussey took Jones' low-key original and turned it into something resembling a power ballad, so it stands out a bit more.

It starts with that marimba, which gives it a light, summery vibe and instantly puts the listener in a good frame of mind. It carries through the verses, lingering in the background without the listener being completely aware of it, but subtly reinforcing that summery feel.

The song has a pretty standard structure of verse, pre-chorus and then chorus – but there's a nifty trick in that each of them (the verse especially) are slightly shorter than expected. Because each element is sung and played differently, it provides distinct textures to *The Horses* which keeps the listener's interest compared to a straight verse-chorus format.

From the verse to the pre-chorus to the chorus there is a steady rise in volume, which creates an emotional lift and anticipation as the chorus approaches; it's not quite the 'quiet verse-loud chorus' format trademarked by Nirvana in *Smells Like Teen Spirit*, but it works.

Braithwaite also sings the hell out of the song, with Urlich's vocals (which are more like a duet than backing vocals) creating a point of difference sonically. They also ensure that the power of Braithwaite's vocals aren't diminished by hearing them constantly throughout the song.

Oh, there's one other thing. *The Horses* actually isn't a short song – it goes for more than four minutes. But it never feels like that, it never feels like it drags. If anything, it feels like it goes by all too quickly.

The hype

Okay, let me tell you a quick story first, about a guy named Marcus Montana. If you were driving almost anywhere in Sydney in mid-1989, you saw the posters; a photo of a moody young man under the slogan 'Marcus is Coming'. They were impossible to miss; this was the 1980s, before councils decided to crackdown on the 'visual pollution' of gig posters. So they were pasted on hoardings, wrapped onto power poles with clear sticky tape, slapped on bus stops, on buses themselves – anywhere they would go.

The Marcus in question was the son of wealthy fruit wholesalers and was either burning away an endowment or was getting the usual 21st birthday present in his family

– whatever he wanted. What Marcus wanted was to be a pop star.

He had a song – *Tell Him I'm Your Man* – as well as a few others and flew to Nashville to record them. It wasn't a *bad* song – I've heard a lot worse – and Marcus had a decent voice, but there wasn't enough there to see the tune rise to the top on its own merits.

When he got back from the Nashville jaunt, he needed a backing band to play live and so got some industry help. It wasn't a shabby band either, as journalist Jack Marx revealed, it included a pre-Whitlams' fame Tim Freedman. "When I heard that it was Marcus – the Marcus from the posters and ads – I thought, 'this is bound to be interesting'," Freedman told Marx. "The ad campaign was a big push that, you would only think, could be paid for by someone like Sony." Plus, the money Marcus' family was paying was good.

Problem for poor Marcus was that the music media had already had a gutful of the 'Marcus is coming' mega hype and were waiting to sink the boot in. And they did. But, not realising the family had already fed Marcus to the wolves, the 'coming' signs were replaced by ones reading "Marcus is here'. The first gig was outside at Darling Harbour, Freedman hiding under a blonde wig.

Up to 1000 people had shown up to check out this Marcus character. And what they saw wasn't great. Not at all. The kid wasn't close to being ready to take the stage. The audience began openly laughing at him.

But he had a tour of Sydney shopping centres to complete, which went as well as you expected they did. And then there was a gig at Selina's, where Marcus was openly mocked by drunk guys getting onstage and playing air guitar next to him.

By this time Montana was well and truly crestfallen, but Freedman talked him into one more gig – at the Lansdowne Hotel. With Marcus a joke in the alternative music community, the crowd turned up to take the piss. From the moment the band started, the audience gave it the full Beatlemania treatment – screaming, trying to touch him, generally going crazy.

As poor Marcus learned too late, you can't *make* a hit happen. You can't put up endless posters and then think 'okay, that's it, job done. We're going to have a hit'. Especially if you're a nobody – people need to react to the song before the performer. He could have spent less effort on plastering posters and more on getting some decent songs.

I tell that story to spell out a simple truth – hype tends to backfire, especially when you don't have the goods to back it up. People don't like being manipulated into liking something. The path a song takes to become popular has to happen organically. *The Horses* didn't get to its iconic status because some promotions company made sure they rammed it down our throats.

It became a much-loved song from the bottom up not the top down. It wasn't record label bosses trying to tell people this was a good song. It was the average punter finding something in the song that resonated with them. They didn't need a poster campaign or having radio stations playing the song on repeat for years to latch onto it.

The meaning

Ricki Lee Jones wrote the song for her daughter Charlotte when she was going through a separation from Charlotte's dad. Hence lyrics like "if you fall I'll pick you up" and "you will grow and until you go I'll be right there by your side". Early on, people had been telling Braithwaite it was about heroin (horse being slang for the drug). He got so concerned he asked the publishers to check with Jones and co-writer Walter Becker just what the song was about. They came back with the news it was about Jones' kid.

Most people would have no idea what the song was about, which actually works to its benefit. The lyrics are sufficiently vague they allow people to attach their own meaning and significance to the song. That's why it can be used to mark the end of a good night, to sing to a lover, to be part of a marriage ceremony or, with the gentle but uplifting tone of the song, even used to farewell someone at a funeral service.

"It gets played at any kind of event because it's so ambiguous," Hussey said. "The meaning of the words 'little darling, way up in the sky' there's a positive aspect of it that can relate to the passing of someone, such as a funeral, or the birth of a new child or your love for the child, a wedding or love for a partner.

"I think that the lyrics are open to interpretation to the individual have made it totally universal."

That's the mark of a good song, one that grow and changes in meaning depending on who is hearing it. Once a songwriter sends a song out into the world, they lose that control and people can make it out to be whatever they want. And sometimes, what it means to them can be more significant than what the song is really about.

The singing

And here I don't mean Braithwaite's singing but those in the crowd at the gig, the pub, the horse races or wherever it's being played. People are suckers for a big singalong at a crowd. It feels good, makes them happy and allows you to put your arm around a mate's shoulder and feel a connection, or even the stranger standing next to you at the gig.

And *The Horses* is pretty easy to sing; it includes all singing types. Even those who can't sing at all. Because Braithwaite kept it vocal lines simple and didn't go crazy with high notes – or speed up the pace too much – he created a song that really lends itself to being sung by a crowd.

Also, it's slow enough that, when a crowd sings it in unison, the words are clear – everyone can keep up and it makes it sound as though it's one voice singing and not hundreds or even thousands. Musically, there are few things that make your hair on the back of your neck stand up than a crowd chorus where you can hear every word.

It hangs around

Remember, this song didn't go screaming up the charts in a week or two. It was five months after *The Horses*' release that it made it to No1. Now what does that tell us about the song?

It's a slow burner – that's what. It's a song that has the quality to stick around for ages without people getting sick of it. It was a song that burrowed into your subconscious and then sat there, as you sung to yourself "that's the way it's gonna be little darling".

That's the sort of quality that has served it well over the years. It show the song can stand the test of time, can stick around without beginning to sound tired or stale. It's a song perfectly built to have this sort of staying power. It was never a flash in the pan, wasn't a song that amused us for a few weeks back in 1991 and was then forgotten.

It was a song that stayed put while others entered the charts one week and disappeared a while later. And while those songs are forgotten, *The Horses* is still with us.

He hangs around too

It's not just *The Horses* that shows resiliency, it's the guy who sings it too. Braithwaite has had more career renaissances than anyone else in the music scene. He's been going since the days of Sherbet more than 40 years ago.

Part of the reason for that is obviously because people liked the stuff he singing. Part of it is because he is truly a nice guy. He's like your cool uncle. It's hard to imagine him pissing off people in the industry or burning bridges.

And part of it is he just keeps going. Even when he was working on that road gang after Sherbet/The Sherbs went kaput, he was still casting an eye to the stage. And through the back half of the 1990s and early 2000s, when Braithwaite couldn't buy a charting hit, he was still out there on the stages of leagues clubs and regional hotels, performing those much-loved tunes.

That's significant because one of those hits was *The Horses*. It wasn't just a song people would hear on the radio or their parents' CDs, it wasn't a song that existed in the past.

It was a song that still lived, still breathed and was still finding an audience. If *The Horses* only existed on CD or Spotify, it wouldn't be the phenomenon it is now. The fact that people could listen to Braithwaite's recording of the song made decades earlier and then go and see him play it live gave it an extra kick that plenty of other hits of the 1990s didn't have.

The crowd

A benefit of being able to go see Braithwaite perform *The Horses* is that you become part of the crowd chorus. Whether you're there with friends and you've got your arms around each other or you went on your own because you couldn't convince your partner to come along, chances are you're singing along.

Sure the first group of people are likely singing louder than the second, but they're all singing. That action forms an attachment to the song that simply doesn't happen if you sit listening to it at home, in the car or on the train.

There's no doubt that being part of a crowd singing along is a thrill. It makes you feel like you're a part of something, like for a few minutes you're in a crowd of friends. It gives you a joyful moment to connect to the song, one which resurfaces every time you hear it. And then reinforces your attachment to *The Horses*.

The bandwagon jumpers

Any time something cool is identified, there will always be latecomers who look to jump on the bandwagon to be part of the cool thing. It's what turns so many singles and albums into hits after the passing of the initial surge where fans all buy a copy. The bandwagoners figure there must be some coolness to having that album, so they go and buy it too.

They're not doing it because they're drawn to how the music makes them feel. Nope, they want to be part of it because they think something cool is going on and they reckon they'll benefit by some of the refracted glow of that cool.

There's probably a bit of that going on with *The Horses* phenomenon. While it was building over a decade, there were a few news stories here and there about it. But it wasn't until around 2018-19 that we saw stories about kids liking *The Horses* and how incredible it was (and there were stories that went the other way of course, as people chose to explain why *The Horses* was a crap song. Which, by then, was a moot point; once people like a song, a rational argument as to why they shouldn't like it just isn't going to work).

Now, as much as I hate giving credit to

bandwagon jumpers, there is a little to hand out. Those people saw those stories about *The Horses*, figured something was happening and chose to jump on the bandwagon – thereby furthering the life of phenomenon.

No guilty pleasure

You may have heard of The Shaggs, a trio made up of sisters Dorothy, Betty and Helen Wiggins. They were forced to form a pop group by dad Austin because when he was a child his mum read his palm and told him he would have daughters who would form a popular music group.

He bought his daughters some instruments (two guitars, a drum kit but no bass for some odd reason) and made them take music lessons and go through tedious hours of rehearsal. He named them The Shaggs and got them gigs in their hometown of Fremont, New Hampshire, in the hope they'd get better.

They didn't, but Austin could not be

stopped. He went and booked them into a studio in 1969, where the engineer tactfully told Austin the kids weren't quite ready. Austin disagreed. "I want to get them while they're hot," he said.

So the engineer hit record on an album of original songs. And they were *terrible* songs. They were totally devoid of any sense of rhythm – especially the drummer – and it always sounded like they weren't actually playing the same song. None of which is at all surprising, given they couldn't play their instruments or sing. You could have recorded any band who were barely acquainted with their instruments and gotten much the same result.

The sisters really had little interest in being a band; they had a Stage Dad who had pushed them into it. So when he karked it, they quickly packed it all in. And that would have been that but in the mid-1970s, it became cool for the hipsters to like The Shaggs, branding their style as outsider art, rather than just crap. Come 1980 and the debut, titled *Philosophy of the World* was re-released and the discordant tunes gained a wider audience. Most of whom liked it did so with a snigger, because of the ineptness of the playing. It was very much filed in the "so bad it's good" category and then they went out to claim some degree of artistic merit in the work, so as to justify their own preference for the music.

Rolling Stone ranked in No 14 all-time in their list of one-album wonders, noting "it takes all of two seconds for the Shaggs' out-rock masterpiece *Philosophy of the World* to fall apart into a glorious, asynchronous mess".

In fact it's hard to find any music press that gives The Shaggs a subpar rating; it's as though praising The Shaggs is one of the criteria a music writer has to tick off before they can be considered a 'serious' reviewer.

I tell the story about The Shaggs because it's an example of the shame felt around liking 'bad' music. The word is in inverted commas because what sort of music is truly 'bad' is totally subjective. Because music doesn't engage with us on a rational level, we're unable to filter out what we think of as 'bad' songs and only listen to the 'good' stuff

Songs don't care whether they're on your list of the worst songs ever recorded, all they want to do is hook you in. That's why we can find ourselves liking a song we've told ourselves it's not cool to like. It's the whole basis of the guilty pleasure; something you enjoy but would be embarrassed were others to find out about it.

One way out of this is to assign some cultural or musical value to the song, thereby turning it from 'bad' to 'good' and allowing you to enjoy it without the fear someone will laugh at you when they see it in your record collection. That's part of what's gone on with The Shaggs; listeners have found themselves enjoying the sounds that they have told themselves should be 'bad' and so have to move the goalposts in such a way as to explain why this group isn't bad while any other band who can't play their instruments *is* bad.

Really, that's no way to live, worrying about the judgment of others when they find out you still like the songs Jason Donovan released just after he left *Neighbours*. The youngsters these days seem to have adopted this concept that's been tagged "post irony" (of course, the youngsters didn't give it that name. Youngsters just do whatever the new, hip thing is and it's to old people to give it a name so they can pretend to understand it). Now, while most older people think everything the kids do is stupid, this post ironic approach is genius. It just means you can like something without having to create some justification for it. You don't have to come up with those crap "it's so bad it's good" excuses or pretend that there is some worth in what it clearly worthless. You're simply allowed to like it because it appeals to you.

So for some of those youngsters getting into *The Horses*, there could be an element of that. They're not worrying whether it's a cheesy song or if their friends will think they're uncool for liking it. They're free to enjoy the tune without having to treat it like a guilty pleasure. Which comes in quite handy when you're prone to singing *The Horses* in public.

Cover versions

Every couple of years, there's an outpouring of shock when someone realises that *The Horses* is – gasp! – a cover version. In 2020 when Braithwaite performed the tune with Chris Sebastian on the finale of *The Voice*, the esteemed *Daily Mail Australia* was surprised to find he didn't actually write the song.

Under the headline '*The Voice Australia* fans are stunned to learn the 'confronting' truth about Daryl Braithwaite's *The Horses*', the online site built a whole story around three tweets from viewers who were shocked to discover that Braithwaite didn't write the song. This is despite the fact Braithwaite has never claimed he did. "Right from when it started I told people I didn't write it, it was Rickie Lee Jones," Braithwaite said. "But I still get people on Facebook going "Daryl, you should give Rickie Lee Jones credit" and I just think: fuck!"

One of the cranky tweets about *The Voice Australia* read "When you realise Daryl Braithwaite made a fortune and career from covering someone else's song...", which is wrong on several levels. Firstly, *The Horses* didn't make him a fortune – all those royalties go to the songwriters. Secondly, Braithwaite's career started in the 1970s, long before *The Horses* came along.

But the funny thing here is that we're getting covers of a cover. In addition to Chris Sebastian, Michael Paynter and Trent Bell both performed the song while contestants on *The Voice*. Taylor Henderson did the same on *X Factor*. And Cody Simpson dressed up as a robot to sing *The Horses* on *The Masked Singer*. Hip hop artist Adrian Eagle performed a version for MTV's *Stripped*.

None of those versions were based on

Ricki Lee Jones' original; they all started with Braithwaite's interpretation. Then there was Vera Blue and Guy Sebastian singing it during Braithwaite's Hall of Fame ceremony. And then there's Client Liaison getting Braithwaite to perform with them at Beyond The Valley. They weren't taking the piss either. "There was no irony whatsoever," said band member Monte Morgan. "We actually try to avoid irony. We genuinely love Daryl. If you had to list Aussie anthems, *The Horses* is right up there with *You're the Voice, Khe Sanh, Solid Rock, Great Southern Land* ... there are only a handful of songs where the entire country knows every single word."

As recently as 2021 even Harry Styles was getting into the song, leading crowds in a singalong during his Australian tour. "I met Harry at the ARIAs, where I sang *The Horses* with Guy Sebastian and Vera Blue. I think that's where he saw the song," Braithwaite said. "He did a good version of it and his audience seemed to like it, that song just keeps finding new audiences."

What all these covers do is simply bolster the popularity of the song. It means those big audiences watching *The Voice* or *The Masked Singer* are being exposed to *The Horses* again and again – and without Braithwaite himself having to perform it. The covers also send the message to listeners that *The Horses* is clearly a popular song – no-one appears on *The X Factor* and performs some unknown song.

All these covers both expose even more people – especially younger people – to the song, keeping *The Horses* in people's ears. Also, they imbue it with a sense of worth ("they're singing it on TV so it has to be good")

So, there you have it. The story of Daryl Braithwaite, *The Horses* and a detailed theory that tries to explain just why the song is so popular. In closing, I'd just like to say it couldn't have happened to a nicer bloke.

Little Darling

BIBLIOGRAPHY

BOOKS

Byrne, David, *How Music Works*, Canongate 2013
Gladwell, Malcolm, *The Tipping Point*, Abacus, 2000
Jenkins, Jeff, *50 Years of Rock in Australia*, Wilkinson Publishing, 2007
Jones, Ricki Lee, *Last Chance Texaco*, Grove Press, 2021
Kruger, Debbie, *Songwriters Speak*, Limelight Press, 2005
Levitin, Daniel, *This is Your Brain on Music*, Atlantic, 2008
Levitin, Daniel, *The World in Six Songs*, Penguin, 2008
Marx, Jack, *Australian Tragic*, Allen & Unwin, 2015
McFarlane, Ian, *The Encyclopedia of Australian Rock and Pop*, Third Stone Press, 2017
Meldrum, Molly, *Ah Well, Nobody's Perfect*, Allen and Unwin, 2016
Meldrum, Molly, *The Never, Um, Ever Ending Story*, Allen and Unwin, 2014

Nichols, David, *Dig: Australian Rock and Pop Music 1960-85*, Verse Chorus Press, 2016
Ryan, Christian, *Rock Country*, Hardie Grant, 2013
Seabrook, John, *The Song Machine*, Vintage, 2015
Street, Andrew P, *The Long and Winding Way to the Top*, Allen & Unwin, 2017
Wilson, Carl, *Let's Talk About Love*, Bloomsbury, 2014
Thompson, Derek, *Hit Makers*, Penguin, 2017
Various, *50 Greatest Australian Artists of All Time*, Rolling Stone, 2021
Various, *The 200 Greatest Australian Albums of All Time*, Rolling Stone, 2022

MAGAZINES AND NEWSPAPERS

Adams, Cameron, 'Four minutes with Daryl Braithwaite', *Herald Sun*, February 18, 2016
Adams, Cameron, 'That's the way it was, little darlin', *The Herald Sun*, May 27, 2016
Adams, Cameron, 'Horses still hits high note', *The Herald Sun*, May 28, 2016
Beach, Camillia, 'Howzat! Australian rock scores a world hit', *The Bulletin*, December 4, 1976

'Big day out for serious punters', *The Herald Sun*, October 27, 2007

'Braithwaite rocks the cup', *The Border Mail*, March 25, 2017

'Braithwaite told to pay $35,000 for management', *The Age*, October 31, 1992

'Braithwaite's joyous footnote to a classic', *The Herald Sun*, April 16, 2017

'Daryl 50 not out – Howzat?', *The Herald Sun*, January 9, 1999

'Daryl scares the horses', *The Herald Sun*, October 26, 2010

'Daryl Braithwaite: singer', *The Age*, January 15, 1993

'Daryl: Higher than before', *Sun-Herald*, January 13, 1991

'Daryl's gambit', *The Sunday Herald Sun*, January 26, 1997

'Daryl's rocky road', *The Herald Sun*, January 17, 2009

'Daryl's winning Edge', *Sun-Herald*, December 31, 1989

Davies, Nathan, 'Daryl, it's time to put The Horses out to pasture', Daily Telegraph, January 3, 2019

'Golden oldies dominate the airwaves of the '90s', *The Age*, December 22, 1994

'Horses to ride again on NYE', *The Herald Sun*, December 28, 2012

'I prostituted myself, says Braithwaite', *Sydney Morning Herald*, August 20, 1992

'Jukebox: The stories behind the song', *The Courier-Mail*, April 22, 2017

'Lucky win on horses', *The Herald Sun*, May 16, 2016

'No angst in these polished pop gems', *The Age*, January 14, 1993

'Riddle that is Braithwaite', *The Mercury* (Hobart), December 30, 2017

'Rock of ages', *Sun-Herald*, May 19, 1991

Schwartz, Larry, 'The demons inside Daryl', *The Sunday Age*, September 1, 1996

'Singer denies trying to cheat men of reward', *The Age*, August 20, 1992

'Solo merit for singer', *Daily Telegraph*, October 19, 2017

'Solo trip to Tassie suits Daryl down to the ground', *Launceston Examiner*, September 30, 2006

'Wild horses can't stop him: that's the way it's gonna be', *The Australian*, April 1, 2017

WEBSITES

Young, David James, 'Daryl Braithwaite Kinda Wishes We'd Get Over *The Horses* Already', Junkee, December 2017

Scrimshaw, Jo, '*The Voice Australia* fans are stunned to learn the 'confronting' truth about Daryl Braithwaite's *The Horses*', Daily Mail Australia, July 20, 2020

PODCASTS

Coffee Chats with Matt Collins, 'Daryl Braithwaite', January 24, 2022

Gavin Wood's Countdown Podcast, 'Daryl Braithwaite', July 23, 2020

Rewind with Steve Bell, 'An oral history of Daryl Braithwaite's The Horses, June 24, 2021

Time to Talk with Sean Sennett, 'Daryl Braithwaite', September 12, 2020

If you liked this book why not check out my others, all which are available through my own micropublishing company Last Day of School?
(www.lastdayofschool.net)

Glen Humphries

Friday Night at the Oxford

The story that led to reunion of legendary band Tumbleweed. An in-depth look at Sunday Painters, a band decades ahead of their time. Iconic shows like HOPE, HyFest and the Steel City Sound exhibition. These are just of the more than 100 stories about Wollongong bands and events written by journalist Glen Humphries for the *Illawarra Mercury*, from 1997 through to 2018, and his own short-lived website Dragster. The 200-plus pages of *Friday Night at the Oxford* provide a snapshot of what happened in the Wollongong music scene over the last 20-odd years – the bands, the venues, the events. It's a celebration of the music of a city.

So dig it.

Little Darling

Healer:
The Rise, Fall and Return of Tumbleweed

With their long hair and fuzzed-up guitars, Tumbleweed rose out of the ashes of late-80s indie band The Proton Energy Pills.

The Wollongong band hit their peak of popularity in the wake of the 1995 album *Galactaphonic*. And then proceeded to shoot themselves in the foot. Guitarist Paul Hausmeister got the sack, and then drummer Steve O'Brien left in protest. From there the band went downhill, releasing albums that met an increasingly uninterested public and playing shows in front of a half-dozen people. So it was no surprise when they called it quits in 2001.

But in 2009 they managed to heal their wounds and reunite, releasing their fifth studio album a few years later and survive the sudden death of bassplayer Jay Curley. Journalist and music writer Glen Humphries has interviewed the members of Tumbleweed numerous times and, in Healer, takes the first complete look at the band's career.

Glen Humphries

Sounds Like an Ending: Midnight Oil, 10-1 and Red Sails in the Sunset

In 1982, Midnight Oil was a band in trouble. Their last album, *Place Without a Postcard*, was supposed to be their big breakthrough but it hadn't worked out that way. So they found themselves in London, feeling the pressure of recording what was a "make or break" album. If this album went the same way as the last one, it could be the end of Midnight Oil. Out of the crisis came *10,9,8,7,6,5,4,3,2,1*, an album that changed everything for the band. It entered the charts and stayed there for more than three years. They started playing bigger venues - and they were able to pay back the bank manager. Two years later, they headed to Japan to record the polarising *Red Sails in the Sunset*. It managed to do what *10-1* couldn't - give the band their first No1 album. In *Sounds Like an Ending*, journalist and author Glen Humphries takes a track-by-track look at these two albums and the times and turmoil that fuelled them.

Little Darling

Alright! Queen at Live Aid

On July 13, 1985, the world tuned in to watch Live Aid beamed in from Wembley in London and John F Kennedy Stadium in Philadelphia. The massive event was spawned from Bob Geldof's idea six months earlier to raise money for Ethiopian famine victims through the release of the charity single, Do They Know It's Christmas?.

The iconic performance on that day came from Queen, a band that had been considering calling it quits just months earlier. Performing in front of an estimated audience of 1.9 billion people, the fourpiece stole the show and revitalised their career.

Alright takes a look back at Queen's performance on that day as well as revisiting the origins of the Band Aid single and the logistics behind getting Live Aid off the ground.

Glen Humphries

Biff
Rugby League's Infamous Fights

For close to a hundred years, the biff has been part and parcel of rugby league. And it was condoned for most of that time. As rough play like stiff arms, high tackles, spear tackles, facials and stomping were weeded out of the game, the punch remained. As recently as the 1980s league bosses would say there was nothing fans liked to see more than two forwards trading blows.

But the biff has all but disappeared in recent years, when the league finally realised there is nothing in the rule book that allows players to punch on. In *Biff*, Glen Humphries looks at some of the most infamous brawls in rugby league, from the Earl Park Riot and a match abandoned after it became a brawl to the most violent grand final and, finally, the punch that changed everything.

Published by Gelding Street Press

Little Darling

The Slab: 24 Stories of Beer in Australia

Beer. You know it and, chances are, you love it. But you might not know the part beer has played in Australian history. Right from the start beer was there. It was on board The Endeavour when Captain Cook set sail for Australia. It was drunk not long after the First Fleet landed in Botany Bay.

It was there when World War I soldiers got a skinful and ran riot in the streets of Sydney. It was there during the era of six o'clock closing where people were still drinking it long after the little hand had passed the six. It was even there when it really shouldn't have been - when Canberra declared itself an alcohol-free zone.

"History as it should be written. With beer. About beer. Crisp. Refreshing. Won't cause bloat."
John Birmingham, author of Leviathan

James Squire: The Biography

After getting caught swiping a few chickens from a neighbour, James Squire was sentenced to seven years in Sydney Cove. You could say it was the best thing he ever did – it led to him become a brewer, policeman, property tycoon, respected citizen and a bloody rich guy. But if all you know about James Squire is what you've read on labels on beer bottles, then you really don't know that much at all.

This book – the first biography of Squire – separates the facts from the well-known myths. Along the way you'll also discover a few other things about Sydney Cove, including Captain Arthur Phillip's efforts to get his hands on some Aboriginal heads for a friend, the early Australian fondness for cider rather than beer, the fight rival brewer John Boston had over a dead pig and the marine who tried to trade his hat for an Aboriginal child.

Night Terrors: The True Story of the Kingsgrove Slasher

Between 1956 and 1959, suburban Sydney was terrorised by a phantom known as the Kingsgrove Slasher. A peeping Tom, he graduated to breaking into houses to watch people sleep before later slashing women and girls with a razor while they lay in their beds.

He punched a 21-year-old woman into unconsciousness, breaking her teeth and cutting her mouth, hit a teenage girl in the face with a piece of wood and slashed a deep wound across the stomach of a 64-year-old woman. The Slasher also groped teens in their beds, and one of his 18 victims was just seven years old.

Night Terrors is the first detailed account of the Kingsgrove Slasher case. It draws on hundreds of newspaper articles written at the time - which show the level of fear in the community - as well as the transcripts from the court hearings, which had been sealed since 1959.

EBOOKS
The Six-Pack: Stories from the World of Beer

From stories of monks making beer, to rumours of an unpleasant secret "ingredient" in a world-famous drink, there are plenty of great stories about beer. And six of them are captured in this ebook.

Beer is Fun!

Oh look, it's the best moments from Beer is Your Friend, the blog that won a national beer writing award and also inspired Dale to leave a comment "give ur self an uppercut u oxygen thief".

Why should you buy this book? Because it's 300-plus and it'll cost you just $2. What else in life will give you loads of entertainment for just $2? Go on, buy it. If you don't like it, I'll give you your money back. Well, that's a lie, I won't give you a cent, because I plan on holidaying in The Bahamas with the $2 you give me.

www.ingramcontent.com/pod-product-compliance
Lightning Source LLC
Chambersburg PA
CBHW040741020526
44107CB00084B/2832